Creativi

Michel Syrett and Jean Lammiman

- Fast track route to fostering and exploiting creativity in any organisation

- Covers the key areas of creative team working and brainstorming, from leading projects with a creative output and choosing and backing winning ideas to motivating and rewarding staff

- Examples and lessons from some of the world's most creative businesses, including AOL Time-Warner, BMW, IDEO and Nortel Networks, and ideas from the smartest thinkers, including Edward de Bono, Gary Hamel, Richard Pascale and W. Chan Kim

- Includes a glossary of key concepts and a comprehensive resources guide

>>EXPRESS EXEC.COM<<
essential management thinking at your fingertips

Copyright © Capstone Publishing 2002

The right of Michel Syrett and Jean Lammiman to be identified as the authors of this work has been asserted in accordance with the Copyright, Designs and Patents Act 1988

First published 2002 by
Capstone Publishing (a Wiley company)
8 Newtec Place
Magdalen Road
Oxford OX4 1RE
United Kingdom
http://www.capstoneideas.com

CIP catalogue records for this book are available from the British Library and the US Library of Congress

ISBN 1-84112-318-8

Printed and bound in Great Britain

This book is printed on acid-free paper

Substantial discounts on bulk quantities of Capstone books are available to corporations, professional associations and other organizations. Please contact Capstone for more details on +44 (0)1865 798 623 or (fax) +44 (0)1865 240 941 or (e-mail) info@wiley-capstone.co.uk

Contents

Introduction to ExpressExec

ExpressExec is 3 million words of the latest management thinking compiled into 10 modules. Each module contains 10 individual titles forming a comprehensive resource of current business practice written by leading practitioners in their field. From brand management to balanced scorecard, ExpressExec enables you to grasp the key concepts behind each subject and implement the theory immediately. Each of the 100 titles is available in print and electronic formats.

Through the ExpressExec.com Website you will discover that you can access the complete resource in a number of ways:

» printed books or e-books;
» e-content – PDF or XML (for licensed syndication) adding value to an intranet or Internet site;
» a corporate e-learning/knowledge management solution providing a cost-effective platform for developing skills and sharing knowledge within an organization;
» bespoke delivery – tailored solutions to solve your need.

Why not visit www.expressexec.com and register for free key management briefings, a monthly newsletter and interactive skills checklists. Share your ideas about ExpressExec and your thoughts about business today.

Please contact elound@wiley-capstone.co.uk for more information.

Introduction to Creativity

» Efficiency is not enough
» Creativity is more than a "nice to have"
» The price of survival should not be blinkered vision

"Organizations did well to employ the most up-to-date equipment, information technology, and management techniques to eliminate waste, defects, and delays. They did well to operate as close as they could to the productivity frontier. But while improving operational efficiency is necessary for achieving profitability, it is not sufficient."

Harvard Business School's Professor Michael Porter, author of the sell-out success *The Competitiveness of Nations*, was speaking at a conference in 1997. He argued that all the efforts organizations take to make themselves "leaner," "process-oriented," and "quality-conscious" help to sustain their ability to compete.

However he also stressed that this was a starting point, not an end in itself. Staying efficient, keeping costs down, delivering products and services on time and to a sufficient standard of quality are goals that merely ensure the organization stays alive. At best, they ensure that the firm is a top player (rather than *the* top player) within its industry.

But measures of this kind won't distinguish any organization from the pack. Moreover, in the long run, if the organization adopts a narrow focus on achieving efficiency and a "zero-error" culture – resulting in a cowed, demotivated, or insecure workforce – while its competitors attract and exploit the creative talent required to break new ground in the sector, these efficiency measures could prove fatal to the firm's future.

It seems odd that as recently as the mid-1990s, creativity was seen as a "nice to have" rather than an essential. Of course nobody admitted as much. The words *innovation* or *innovative* were sprinkled liberally across corporate annual reports and PR statements. But the actions needed to ensure that creativity was seeded and nurtured throughout the whole organization and not just the Board (if that) were often not in place.

No more vivid illustration of this exists than the business issues and concerns raised by the events of September 11, 2001. At the time of writing (some weeks later), it was unclear whether the collapse in consumer confidence that these events provoked in industries like air travel and tourism would in turn lead to a full-blown recession in 2002. Regardless of where the crisis in world events leads, however, an atmosphere of uncertainty is settling on the business communities of the developed world.

Already, innovation and creativity – which have dominated board-room thinking during the last decade – are spiraling down the business agenda as senior managers focus on survival and cutbacks. Yet the experience of the last recession suggests that this is the time when creative minds are most needed.

Large corporations mostly stand still in their thinking during a recession. The world does not. During the recession of the early 1990s, the technology that led to the Internet revolution became universally available while a new generation of young people with new consumer tastes and radically different career expectations came of age.

Corporations that had led their industries in the 1980s, like IBM and Marks & Spencer, entered the new boom of the mid-1990s with a perspective of the world that had been frozen in aspic – and paid the price. What went wrong was not the excellence of their processes or the technology and their disposal but their collective frame of mind.

Californian guru Richard Pascale's study of long-term survivors like Sears, Shell, and the US Army has made him an expert in corporate longevity. Speaking at a conference in Prague in 1997, he commented:

> "The fact is that most organizations, as a consequence of their size and age, drift into a condition in which people's relationship to power is one of resignation. Consciously or not, people look at their own power to bring about results and draw the conclusion that nothing new is possible and the power to make change is not 'in their turf.'"

Until the technology depicted in Stephen Spielberg's film *AI (Artificial Intelligence)* becomes a reality, business creativity will remain centered around the relationship between the organization and the series of individuals that make up their workforce. Our own research, conducted for Roffey Park Institute in the UK (see Chapter 2 and Chapter 8), suggests that the ideas that "spark" breakthroughs in products and services only achieve their full potential through the collective effort and resources of the organization. But the inspiration that "ignites" that spark is entirely individual.

Richard Pascale argues this inspiration is only inflammable by increasing workers' "sense of possibility." If we factor in Michael Porter's argument that it is creativity that distinguishes the market leaders rather than simply the excellence of their processes, then there never has been a time when sustaining it has more importance. Many people's sense of what is possible has been undermined in the uncertainty that has followed the events of September 11, 2001. Restoring it is the most important challenge for business leaders in the early years of the new decade.

What is Creativity?

Ask most people to define creativity as a generic term and they will nearly always think of some form of solitary artistic endeavor. Whether it be Shakespeare's *Sonnets*, Beethoven's *Fifth*, or Van Gogh's *Sunflowers* that springs to mind, the struggle by an individual to make his or her vision of the world real is readily understood and envisaged. "My paintings bring me nothing but pain," said the British painter Turner, in a well-known description of creative frustration. "The reality is so immeasurably below the conception."

IN SPACE, NO ONE CAN HEAR YOU SCREAM (ALONE)

Yet in the performing arts, and the multi-media industries spawned by the twentieth century, creativity is nearly always a collective process. Hollywood blockbuster films are a good example. The 1979 sci-fi hit *Alien*, which has spawned three sequels and inspired as many decades of new film-makers, was not the product of a single mind.

The basic concept – a small number of crew members on a spaceship are threatened by an alien creature that has somehow got on board and is running around in the shadows picking them off one by one – originated from the writer/designer duo Dan O'Bannon and Ron Cobb. The pair had made the cult classic *Dark Star* in the early 1970s, which pioneered the idea of "used space" – space where, as on earth, nothing works and everything goes wrong – as an antithesis to the idealistic vision of space travel depicted in Stanley Kubrick's *2001: Space Odyssey*. But *Dark Star* had been a comedy. Now they wanted to produce a horror film from the same starting point.

They approached 20th Century Fox who were keen to follow up on the unexpected success of *Star Wars*, which had been released two years before. Fox teamed O'Bannon with a co-writer, Ron Shusett. He came up with one of the key breakthroughs in the script: that the alien gets onto the ship by impregnating one of the crew, something which, because it entails a form of bodily violation or "rape," gives the finished film much of its threatening psycho-sexual power.

The "look" of the film, the second key breakthrough, was the result of a creative collaboration between the man brought in to direct it, Ridley Scott, who had a background in graphic design and advertising; and the Swiss graphic artist H.R. Giger, who published a cult sci-fi magazine called *Ecronicon*, which depicted strange hybrid creatures that were part organic and part robotic. It was Giger who created the designs for the "alien" and the disturbing industro-organic sets of the alien's planet.

The success of the series as a whole was ensured, not without a lot of artistic compromise, by the appointment of executive producer David Giler – and also by the continuing commitment and creative input of the lead star Sigourney Weaver, whose character Ripley had become, by the end of the first film, an essential feature of any sequel.

Break down and analyze the processes and roles involved in making *Alien* and they compare very closely with those of almost any other creative project in business. Ruth McCall, founder and former managing director of Cambridge Animation Systems, a company launched in 1991 to provide software for cartoon feature films, argues that getting a software team to write a good product is the same as making a film or even getting the *corps de ballet* to perform their routine. Whatever the differences in the output or goal, they all involve a lot of communication and co-ordination so that the whole, when it emerges, is complete.

KEEPING THE SPARK ALIGHT

This is confirmed by our own study of creative projects in organizations as varied as a large airline, an international aid charity, an international military headquarters, and a dot-com startup (see Chapter 8).

One or two individuals usually "spark" off the process with an idea that is generally only a starting point for discussion. The process of taking this germ for an initiative and turning it into a successful commercial project is undertaken by managers playing four very different roles.

» *Sponsors*: the people who promote the idea or project inside the organization, ensuring that it is not dismissed and who sustain interest in it during lean times. This role is commonly played by senior line managers, members of the board, or non-executive directors.
» *Shapers*: the people who make the idea or project "real," using their creativity to flesh out the premise and/or to find the practical means to meet its objectives. This role is most commonly played by members of the project team appointed to implement the idea, process-oriented consultants, and R&D staff from key suppliers.

» *Sounding boards*: the people outside the project upon whose objectivity and broader knowledge of the field can be drawn to inform and validate the premise or to comment on the practicalities. This role is often performed by informal or formal members of an individual's personal or professional network, trusted colleagues or company-appointed mentors, strategy-oriented consultants, academics, or researchers in the field.

» *Specialists*: the people who draw on their specialist knowledge or skills to shape the idea or project from a specific standpoint, often using the opportunity to break new ground in their own field. This role is often played by members of the project team, consultants (process and strategy), academics, researchers, and R&D staff from key suppliers.

Taking the concept for *Alien* as an illustration of these roles in practice, the "sparks" were Dan O'Bannon and Ron Cobb, the creators of *Dark Star*. Their idea of a horror film depicting "used space" was the starting point. But the idea they submitted to 20th Century Fox was only half evolved. They had evolved the idea of an alien creature picking off a small number of crew members in a ship traveling in deep space, but they had not worked out how it had got onto the ship, and they had no sense of what it would look like.

Under the guidance of executive producer David Giler, who acted as "sponsor," several "shapers" were brought in. The most important was the director Ridley Scott, whose background in advertising and graphic design gave him a sense of what the film would look like. He in turn hired the Swiss graphic artist H.R. Giger, who drew on his work *Ecronicon* to design the "alien" and the look of the alien planet.

Another important "shaper" was co-writer Ron Shusett who (apparently on waking up in the middle of the night) suggested the key concept of the alien impregnating human beings as a means of procreation, thus solving the problem of how it got onto the ship. Finally there were a variety of "specialists" and "sounding boards" who turned these visions into reality, most importantly the line producer Ivor Powell, the film editor Tony Rawlings, and the actors, of which one, Sigourney Weaver, became a sponsor and shaper in her own right in the sequels.

The interplay between the key players on what most people would see as the ultimate "creative" project is no different to what might occur in a commercial initiative in a less glamorous industry. In 1998, British Airways opened a new state-of-the-art headquarters designed specifically to foster serendipity between staff from different departments and thus eliminate the turf wars that had been such a handicap in the run up to privatization in the late 1980s. Although the future of the building was in some doubt at the time of writing, because of the crisis in the airline industry provoked by the events of September 11, 2001, this remains one of the most ambitious projects ever undertaken with this purpose.

The seeds of the idea were planted 10 years before in the mind of the then general manager of property, Gwilym Rees-Jones, who was tasked with the job of finding new space to accommodate an overspill of staff from BA's then headquarters building Speedbird House.

A lack of leasable property led Rees-Jones to opt for the idea of BA buying vacant land and purpose-building their own headquarters. He immediately realized that this would be a heaven-sent opportunity to change the way people worked, thus providing a people vision for the project rather than making it a purely technical construction task. It took him five years to get the Board to agree and the one word that he used to describe the personal quality he needed most is the one word also used by *Alien* co-writer Dan O'Bannon in persisting in looking for a studio to film his script: "stubbornness."

However, like O'Bannon in the *Alien* sequels, Rees-Jones did not see the project through to completion. Once the idea was taken up, Rees-Jones was promoted to oversee planning for London Heathrow Airport's proposed fifth terminal. His ideas and vision for the new headquarters was taken up by Chris Byron, whose role in managing the team that designed and constructed it has extraordinary parallels with that played by Ridley Scott on the *Alien* set.

The teamwork is described in greater detail in Chapter 7 but it is worth stressing here that the creative interplay between Byron and the Norwegian architect Neils Torp – brought in to design Waterside – mirrors that between Scott and the Swiss graphic artist H.R. Giger. Torp and Giger were both "creatives" with an uncompromising vision of what they wanted to achieve in conceptual terms.

They both had to be persuaded, sometimes on a day-to-day basis, to make compromises in the interests of both cost and commercial realism. In the end, disputes over conceptual design prompted Scott to restrict Giger to design the sets for the alien planet while bringing in another designer to do the sets for the spaceship. A rather similar compromise was reached between Byron and Torp when Torp – a former town planner who had pioneered the idea of commercial buildings as "corporate villages" – tried to insist that there should be no computer terminal points in the social areas of BA's headquarters. Byron insisted that there had to be terminals in all parts of the building to foster the kind of virtual working BA wanted to achieve, but suggested they be positioned so that people using them faced everybody else.

THE PROCESS IS THE THING

What we learn from this is that the right methodology is important to whether organizations fully exploit their creative potential. The language used in any creative exchange, the perspective of the participants, the responses given to new and often wild ideas, and the "thinking" that underpins the management culture will all help to determine whether the flow of ideas that lead to creative breakthroughs is opened up or shut down.

Equally important is the attitude of management. Whether line managers see it as their responsibility to foster and champion the ideas of their subordinates, whether someone is on hand to act as a sounding board or mentor, and whether there is a blame culture which punishes people who take risks that fail will all influence whether an individual feels enabled to bring his or her insight and perspective to the work table or use it elsewhere – either in their leisure activities or to start up a venture of their own. There is also a definable process to any creative project and managers have specific ways of intervening at their disposal to ensure that the twin goals of creativity and commercial reality are kept in balance.

As Cambridge Animation Systems' Ruth McCall concludes: "Business creativity is about how you work with people, how people work in groups, how people manage change, how people get control of their working lives, and how well they are able to integrate their working lives into their whole life." The next chapters will explore these issues in greater depth.

KEY LEARNING POINTS

» Most modern creative projects are collective. One or two individuals may "spark" off the process but the ideas that make the project "real" come from a variety of other people at various stages of the project.

» The roles played are very varied. They include "sponsors" who champion the idea in senior circles and gain backing for it; "shapers" who build on the initial concept; "sounding boards" who give impartial advice; and a variety of "specialists" who add their own thinking from a highly focused standpoint.

» Creativity is, therefore, governed by specific processes and interventions that managers can draw on to ensure that the twin goals of innovative ideas and commercial realities are kept in balance.

The Evolution of Creativity as a Business Concept

» The old priority: the selection and retention of an elite
» The new priority: the transformation of the whole organization
» Opening up visual and lingual horizons
» Creativity in a recession: learning from the past

The value of creative thinking in business is self-evident. From the point that management became a recognized discipline in the late nineteenth century, the objective of using the right techniques to foster innovation in the organization was a key goal of the new profession. "Under scientific management," wrote the first great management guru, Frederick Taylor, in 1911 "the initiative and ingenuity of the workmen can be obtained with absolute regularity, while even the best of the older type of supervision, this level of initiative is only obtained spasmodically and somewhat irregularly ..."

However until the start of the 1990s, when the idea of organizations having collective skills revolutionized business strategy, creativity was an attribute that was seen to apply more to some individuals and industries than to others.

NATURE RATHER THAN NURTURE

In the case of individuals, for example, creativity was something that you were assumed to be born with – or that you acquired at an early age. The influx of a new cadre of psychologists into key personnel and business school faculty posts during the 1960s and 1970s reinforced this view.

The prevailing research method of the day, when analyzing key management skills, was to pick a group of people with a successful track record and see what they had in common. In the 1988 study *High Flyers: An Anatomy of Managerial Success* by Charles Cox and Cary Cooper, top-flight chief executives were found to have sound analytical and problem-solving skills: to be able see "the wood for the trees." They were also found to have a high level of innovation, defined by the authors as

"the sort of people who in making changes would not be constrained by the existing system, but would challenge existing procedures and assumptions, thus producing something *new* [their italics] rather than [a] modification of what currently exists."

In a similar study conducted at about the same time, Marsha Sinetar of the Massachusetts Institute of Technology studied a controlled group of people she identified as creative entrepreneurs working in organizations. Examining a cadre of people who had proven entrepreneurial skills but who remained salaried staff, she found that they thrived – to a far greater extent than other employees – on the freedom to pursue their own ideas and ways of working. At the same time, she found that this singular thinking often undermined their ability to work in teams, supervise other staff, or lead the organization.

The implication of these studies is that managing creativity is primarily a recruitment and appraisal challenge. There is a definable group of people either inside or outside the organization who *are* creative, in the sense that they possess certain skills and personal attributes that are either inherent or have been acquired at an early age. The key is to spot them early and keep them as long as you can.

As a distinct cadre, with their own idiosyncratic foibles and behaviors, they also need to be managed in a distinct way. Journals in the late 1980s and early 1990s were full of articles about how to manage "creative" workers, drawing largely on the methods used by companies in what are deemed to be creative industries: advertising, public relations, the arts, broadcasting, and design.

In an article called "Blessed be the new creation," UK advertisement agency head Winston Fletcher, for example, drew on the experiences of his own industry to say:

"Probably the most important in the motivation of creatives is that – compared to others – remuneration is not an important factor. This is not to say creatives are not interested in money, far from it. However there appears to be no correlation whatsoever between the money they earn and the resulting quality of their work. Unless they are piece-workers, they cannot be persuaded to work harder by being paid more. The best creatives get the most money but the money is paid to them for their talent, not to motivate them."

Similarly, a US article "Strategies for managing creative workers" advised:

"Freedom to express themselves isn't enough to keep creative workers productive. If you ask any of them what sounds the death knell of creativity, chances are they'll say "structure" – rules and regulations, endless rounds of approval, strict dress codes, hard-and-fast office hours, rigid assignments, and fill-in-the-blank paperwork. Therefore if you want your creatives to perform to the best of their ability, loosen the corsets that bind your corporation."

This approach sat very well in an era when the pursuit of "high flyers" was practically a boardroom obsession and a parallel hunt for "creatives" could be latched onto the personnel wizardry and mystique that surrounded the process.

However, it suffered from the same flaws. As a recruitment expert commented in 1988:

"Telling a small part of the workforce it has talent, creative or otherwise, is very like telling the rest that they lack it. Targeted recruitment and focused development aimed at spotting and 'bringing on' people perceived to be high flyers or creatives seeps deep into the culture of the organization and are bound to produce elitist beliefs about what kind of development are valued, and for whom."

THE UNIVERSAL GOOD

The shift in the last decade has been from seeing creativity as a distinct set of skills and personal characteristics possessed by a small number of elite workers who should be treated differently from everyone else, to seeing it as a collective capability that the whole organization can embrace.

The concept of core capabilities originated with an academic duo, Gary Hamel from London Business School and his long-time partner C.K. Prahalad from the University of Michigan, in a much acclaimed book *Competing for the Future,* published in 1994.

The book, which in classic fashion developed out of a landmark article in *Harvard Business Review,* carried two powerful messages: first, that the sustainable health of a business cannot be achieved by simply applying an accountant's rule to costs; and second, that managers need to look much further into the future, examining not only the skills or capabilities that make their organizations unique today but also those that will make it unique in the next decade.

This uniqueness is, according to Hamel, collective. It is founded in the culture of the organization, the way it operates and the way it communicates, rather than in the creative skills of a few highly placed executives. The companies that succeed are those that understand their strengths or "core competencies" and use them to revolutionize their industries by, for example, "radically improving the value equation" (for example, like the US company Fidelity Investments, which lowered the entry level to foreign equity funds to allow a slice of the action to customers of modest means), "striving for individuality" (as Levi Strauss did when they offered tailored or personal pairs of jeans) or "increasing accessibility" (for example, direct telephone banking).

What emerged from this new approach to strategy was the idea that the creative capability of the organization is shaped by the way the whole workforce works and feels about the organization. One of Hamel's colleagues at London Business School, Professor John Stopford, argues that the confidence managers have in themselves, their company, and their role in the company has a direct bearing on their ability to develop new ways of thinking that lead to innovative solutions.

In a program in 1997 designed to promote a shared view of the future among the 300 most senior managers of the pharmaceuticals giant GlaxoWellcome (before the merger with SmithKline Beecham that formed GlaxoSmithKline), the whole of the second week, conducted at the Fuqua Business School at Duke University in South Carolina, focused on each individual manager, the kind of company he or she wanted to build, and what part he or she would have in building it.

In a similar exercise conducted for a British insurance company, London & Edinburgh, at the time owned by ITT, Stopford asked divisional managers and members of the strategic management group where they felt their company was in the international competitive league and where they expected it to be in five years' time.

Both exercises were conducted under the auspices of programs designed to make each company more innovative and capable of responding effectively to a quickly changing industry. Both were designed from the standpoint that there is a direct link between an organization's creative capability and the way all its managers and workers think, see, and feel about the firm and their role in it.

In this sense, creativity at the start of the twenty-first century is more of an organization development challenge than a recruitment and career management task. Its foundations lie less on the high flyer programs of the 1960s and 1970s, which focused on recruiting and developing a creative elite, and more on the change management strategies of the 1980s and 1990s, which aimed to foster a loyalty and enthusiasm among the whole workforce that would in turn prompt all employees, either in teams or as individuals, to tackle emerging or long-standing challenges more creatively.

MIND GAMES

While there is still recognition that some individuals work more creatively than others, and that there is an important role for "hot groups" and think tanks made up from people with a creative track record, this is tempered by a new realization that a person's creative potential is more to do with how they respond to the environment around them than by early life or work experiences.

As the following chapters will illustrate, the most important academic work and corporate initiatives in this field have been in exploring how organizations can re-shape the way people work and the space they work in to help foster their creativity. This covers issues such as how teams and individuals creatively interact, what kind of workspace is best suited to, say, individual reflection as opposed to serendipitous exchanges and what role managers and supervisors should play to foster and champion the ideas of their subordinates.

There is also a recognition that the most creative breakthroughs often occur when people look at a common business problem from a different perspective. Trying to broaden how individuals *see* both their organization and their work has become a new focus in business education.

The result has been an outpouring of courses, programs, articles, and books looking at business from a multitude of different standpoints. These cover the re-interpretation or re-examination of the function of business or the role of management from, for example, the perspective of the works of Shakespeare and Proust, the philosophies of Machiavelli and Descartes, the strategies of Sun Tzu and Clausewitz, the scientific standpoint of physicists and anthropologists, and the techniques of actors, athletes, and (yes, believe it!) horse whisperers.

The true value of this kind of lateral thinking has yet to be fully realized, largely because the lessons drawn from these initiatives are often second-hand and taken too literally (see Chapter Six). Richard Dawkins, the eminent UK scientist responsible for much of the research work on the alpha male, highlighted in his best-selling book *The Selfish Gene*, published a much-needed article in *Harvard Business Review* in 2001, pointing out that scientists' opinions about the relevance of their work to business management counted for very little and that their only role was to trigger an individual train of thought that was personal to each reader.

However, one by-product has been a spotlight on the black and white thinking that often cuts short creative thought in the workplace. Physicists like Danah Zohar and psychologists like Daniel Goleman point out that the roots of business management lie in the university lecture halls and professional tutorial rooms of the late nineteenth century, which were heavily steeped in the philosophies of either Newton or Aristotle, depending on your chosen discipline.

Newtonian and Aristotleian thought heavily influenced the concept of scientific management, pioneered by F.W. Taylor, which dominated business in the early twentieth century and which still shapes the principal professions – law, accountancy, engineering, banking – which are the recruiting grounds for senior managers.

It paints the forces shaping the workplace as simple, law abiding, and ultimately controllable. It also places a high premium on rationality and analysis and on there being a "right" path to any goal.

This contrasts and conflicts with "quantum" thinking based on the work of Einstein and Hawking, which paints the world as complex, chaotic, and perpetually uncertain and which promotes thinking based on paradox, ambiguity, and the fact that there are many valid paths from A to B.

It also conflicts with the work of the 1960s psychologist Alex Osborn and his more illustrious successor Edward de Bono, which suggested that we are all sitting on a "volcano" of ideas that are only prevented from pouring out into the open by our self-doubts and the criticism of others. Off the wall or unworkable ideas are often the most valuable because they get other people to think outside their box and act as a bridge to new frames of thought.

CHANGING GEAR, NOT BRAKING

As this book was on the point of going into production, the early signs of a recession in North America and Europe were taking their toll on innovation as a key business goal. But as we argued in Chapter 1, economic uncertainty is the time when creative thinking is most needed. Corporations tend to stand still in their thinking but the technological and social change that drives business innovation carry on and, if anything, intensify.

Conventional wisdom makes it hard to believe that there is very much an organization can do to sustain a creative culture during a period of job cuts and cost or promotion freezes. But in Chapter 6 we highlight a number of ways in which managers can sustain creative thinking during periods of uncertainty.

A popular management topic during the last decade was chaos theory: the concept that adversity breeds invention, or as the Californian guru Richard Pascale puts it: "Contention does more than make us creative. It makes us whole, it propels us along the journey of development." The last recession seemed, by contrast, to prove Harvard professor Dorothy Leonard's observation that the opposite of harmony is not tension but apathy. It will be interesting to see whether 10 years of focus on innovation will bring any difference.

KEY LEARNING POINTS

» The key point of debate is whether some people are more creative than others. The belief that this is the case has led organizations, until recently, to treat creativity as a recruitment and retention issue. Spotting and nurturing a small elite of creative thinkers was the main focus.

» More recently, the idea that organizations have collective "capabilities" has focused more attention on how the right work environment and relationship can enable all workers to be more creative. This has led organizations to re-examine issues like workspace design, flexible working practices, and the effective use of new technology.

» Economic uncertainty need not lead to a total "freeze" in creative thought. Indeed, times of crisis are where it is most needed. There are ways in which organizations can make the necessary cutbacks yet sustain innovative thinking (see Chapter 6).

TIMELINE

A timeline follows, showing the emergence of creativity as a business concept.

Timescale	Prevalent Philosophy	Originators
Early twentieth century	Initiative and ingenuity seen to be achievable as a by-product of "scientific" management	F.W. Taylor, Frank and Lillian Gilbrethe
1950s and 1960s	Concepts of lateral mindedness and "out of box" thinking are pioneered in business – but generally only among senior managers	Alex Osborn, Francis Vaughan, Edward de Bono, John Frank
1970s and 1980s	The age of the "high flyer": creativity as a "peculiar" capability to be identified, selected, and nurtured in specific individuals	Cary Cooper, Marsha Sinetar, Charles Cox

(continued overleaf)

(*Continued*)

Timescale	Prevalent Philosophy	Originators
Mid-1990s	The age of organizational "competencies": creativity as a collective capability to be shaped through better work environment and team skills	Gary Hamel, Richard Pascale, Michel Syrett and Jean Lammiman
Late-1990s	Research into the "whole brain": IQ tempered by emotional and spiritual intelligence	Michael Jensen, Chris Argyris, Daniel Goleman, Danah Zohar

The E-Dimension of Creativity

The almost universal take-up of e-mail and Internet in the business world since the beginning of the 1990s has sparked two revolutions that span the issues raised by this title. The first of these revolutions concerns how creative exchanges inside organizations are undertaken. This is covered in depth in the counterpart chapter to this one in the ExpressExec title *The Innovative Individual*. The second revolution is in what creative thought has generated in the way of new products and services available by e-commerce, an evaluation radically transformed by the dot-com crash in the latter half of 2000. This is the subject of this chapter.

CAXTON AND MOUSE

The rise and (temporary) fall of the dot-coms provides a perfect case-study in how creative thinking is applied to a given challenge or opportunity. In the late 1990s, the terms *innovation* and *creativity* were seen as synonymous with *any* use of e-commerce. No self-respecting journalist or business writer would publish a book or article on the subject without at least one dot-com case-study or profile of a dot-com millionaire (the latter usually young and straight out of college).

There was no shortage of commentators to point out that the arrival of e-commerce was a watershed in how trade is conducted, on a scale comparable only with the arrival of the printing press in the fifteenth century. In a lecture at London Business School in 1997 the god-figure of new technology, president of the Intel Corporation Andy Groves, argued that the arrival of the Internet was the perfect example of a "strategic inflection point" (see Chapter 1): a moment in any organization's life when a change in strategy is required which will be difficult or impossible to implement further down the line if it is not detected at its inception.

However, Grove was quick to make the following caveat:

> "I think that everybody agrees theoretically that the Internet will change everything. But we will not agree when it will change each individual business. Act on it too early and your market will not be ready for what you have to offer. Act on it too late and your competitors may have stolen a march on you. This process of 'is it the right time or isn't it?' is occupying us all at the moment."

Grove has put his finger on a key piece of the creative jigsaw that is bedeviling senior managers right now. The crash of technology stocks during the second half of 2000, where large Internet firms saw their share prices on the NASDAQ index fall by 90 percent from their peak value the previous spring, with hundreds more falling by more than half, has led some commentators to argue that the "new" economy is a fiction, and that the Internet's significance as a strategic factor in business thinking had been wildly exaggerated in the mid-1990s.

But this is swinging the pendulum too far the other way. "It wasn't real then and it isn't real now," commented Glen Meake, chief executive of Freemarket – one of many Internet stock market fireworks in 2000 – soon after the crash, implying that his and other firms were absurdly overvalued before the slump and irrationally undervalued after it. As he went on to argue, the real issue is whether firms are using the new technology to transform "the proposition" they are offering their clients or merely refine it.

ACCESS VERSUS RICHNESS

The message was taken up by Eric Salama, group strategy director of the international marketing services group WPP, in a second lecture on the new economy at London Business School held in September 2001, four years after the first given by Andy Grove.

Like Glen Meake, Salama distinguishes in creative terms between those companies that are using technology to change fundamentally what they are offering their customers and those that are merely delivering electronically what they previously delivered through other methods. But he stresses that the key factor here is recognizing how fast and to what extent the expectations of the organization's customers are themselves being changed by their use of Internet and related technologies.

There is, he argues, drawing on theories outlined in a recent book *Blown to Bits*, a play-off between "richness" – by which he means the establishment of a highly personalized relationship with the customer, usually involving human contact over the phone or face-to-face – and "easy access" in any business transaction.

Much of the first wave of dot-com companies exploited the new technology by providing customers with easy access. Lastminute.com and Amazon.com both did this, playing on the fact that people didn't want to waste time setting up and attending a face-to-face meeting or even a phone call to make simple cost-based purchases they could just as easily make at the click of a mouse.

But there are transactions where "richness" is still an essential customer requirement and where transactions over the Net will not provide it. The creative twist is assessing just how much richness is required, in what form and how this is likely to change over what period of time.

As Salama says

"Let's take financial services as an example. Ten years ago, most people would insist on seeing a representative from the company if they were buying a mortgage. Now, a growing number of people don't feel the need. They will use the Net to shop around to find the best supplier offering the most advantageous rate. But, nonetheless, most people will want a human being to speak to at the end of a phone before they make the deal and this is likely to remain the case for some time. This is why banks like First Direct, whose transactions are based on phone contact, are still rated more highly in terms of customer service than banks where transactions are conducted entirely on-line. The information I need could be provided through the computer but it is a comfort factor to speak to someone.

"However, if I am a well-heeled professional with a stock portfolio that needs managing, and trust and confidence in the individual is a key factor, this is a different matter entirely. I will want to get a feel for the manager's know how, experience, and integrity and this, at least for the moment, requires at least one and maybe regular meetings because the way I assess all this is likely to be as much through tacit signals as what he or she has to say.

"Having said this, what we are finding at WPP is that it may be possible to provide even this level of richness using technological means in a few years' time. We have a stake in a company called Imagine which is developing sophisticated voice-over and video-over IP technology that will enable me to conduct visual conversations with, say, my asset manager at the click of a button.

Personally, I would still feel it important to meet the individual at least once but after that the technology would serve. But – who knows in an age when people get married over the Net – this too may change over time. The key for any business is whether assessing their customers' expectations in terms of richness and how it is delivered is ahead or behind the company's technology and what it can offer."

THE CUSTOMER AS EMPLOYEE

The issue facing businesses that use new technology as a medium for creative breakthroughs in new products and services for their clients is therefore identical to the one they confront in using it as a medium for creative exchanges between their staff. It is all down to the comfort factor of the individual.

In the chapter on the e-dimension in the ExpressExec title *The Innovative Individual*, we highlight the fact that individuals' willingness to use e-mail, intranets, and the Web as fora for interactive dialog is by no means uniform. The issue raised by Eric Salama – that customer relationships where trust and confidence are critical still need to be founded in the tacit language that comes from mutual eyeballing – is mirrored in the personal ice-breaking that needs to take place in creative team building and project management.

Similarly, the emergence of a new breed of professionals that have been handling computers since they were in diapers and, in tandem, video conferencing and voice-over IP technology that make electronic exchanges more "real," are both making virtual exchanges inside organizations as intimate and acceptable as the electronic dialog that underpins relationship marketing and customer service.

CASE STUDY: GMT GAMES

One of the most important gateways of the latest Web technology is that it opens up the possibility of dialog with customers at every stage of development of new products, services, or propositions: from inception and early experimentation to trial testing and feedback.

This is particularly effective when the customer base is small, highly specialized, but disparately located. Recognizing this fact has played a key role in helping GMT Games, a manufacturer of historical and military board games based in California, revolutionize the way it conducts its market research and product development.

GMT was founded by veteran game designer Gene Billingsley and graphic artist Rodger B. MacGowan in 1990. Few people in the games industry would have ascribed good prospects to a company specializing solely in board games in this particular field. The older generation of history-based board game fans that had underpinned the industry in the previous three decades appeared to have lost interest, and most of the new generation were attracted more to computer fantasy games like *Tomb Raider* and *War Hammer*.

However, Billingsley calculated – shrewdly as it has turned out – that the veteran historical gamers had not lost interest in the hobby because they had "grown out" of it: it was simply that they were bored with the games on offer that had become, in the late 1980s, over-complex, poorly designed, and targeted at "anoraks": over-obsessive, cliquey people who could spend hours on their hobby because they had precious little else to do in their lives.

Billingsley and MacGowan wanted to recapture the mainstream market with better designed games that were more fun and dynamic and could be played both alone and between friends in the context of a routine social life, rather than solely in the clubs and conventions that had been the mainstay of the industry in the previous decade.

However, within five years of launching the company, they started to face problems. MacGowan had partnered with Billingsley in the first place because he had business sense as well as an interest in the hobby. Company after company in the industry had gone bust because the founders failed to appreciate that, in a niche market where products require painstaking design and high production values, accurately assessing the likely demand and time to market is the difference between life and death.

Games aimed at a mass market, such as *Monopoly* or *Risk*, very quickly turn into "cash cows" because people go on buying them year in and year out. But historical gamers have specialist tastes. They like particular periods of history and their tastes are constantly in flux, not least because the last 10 years has seen a renaissance in historical and military writing and broadcasting, which has generated a demand for games covering previously uncharted periods. Keeping track of this demand is not easy. The cost of designing and producing games of this kind, and the cash flow implications, means one "turkey" can kill a manufacturer almost overnight.

By the mid-1990s, the early success of the company meant that they had fueled a demand for more games and were receiving a plethora of proposals from either in-house or independent designers for new games to cover everything from Greek mythology to the fighting in Bosnia. The extremely disparate nature of the marketplace, and the fact that fewer of the mainstream customers attended clubs and conventions (the traditional fora for market research), made it very hard for GMT to assess which games were likely to catch on fast and which would take so long to yield a return that it would endanger the company's financial future.

So in 1997 Billingsley and MacGowan sat down with one of their associate designers, Tony Curtis, and came up with a new initiative which they called Project 500 (P500). The idea was that details of games "in embryo" would be posted to their regular subscribers, who would be invited to make credit card orders at a discount up front. This would provide the company with the finance it needed to produce the game. Billingsley calculated that 500 pre-orders would be sufficient to cover the costs of design and production and at the point when the company received the magic number, the game would go into production. In essence, they were reversing the conventional R&D relationship by letting the customers decide what games they were to produce rather than the designers.

To get customers to "buy into" the idea, however, required that they see a level of detail that would be difficult to achieve using conventional mail order materials. So the trio significantly upgraded the technology they were using on their Website. Using the new-age JPEG files, the Website can now provide highly detailed full-color reproductions of the components of "work in progress" such as rules, maps, counters, and playing cards.

Originally intended solely to fuel P500 pre-sales, this technology has now taken the company into entirely new territory. Subscribers to the Website are not only able to influence which games GMT produces but – by commenting on the components on view when they are still being worked on by the designers – are now involving themselves directly in the product's design.

Describing the dynamic this creates, Rodger MacGowan comments:

"The clear, full-color examples of maps, counters, cards and other components not only help stimulate P500 pre-sales. They allow customers to comment on whether they think the 'feel' and design of the game is right, which in turn enables the designer to adjust and improve in the work in progress.

"The Website also includes a regularly updated letter from the president – 'News From Gene' – which creates a human contact with the company. Through these updates they get to know what we are thinking, what we are concerned about and, because the medium is interactive, how they can help us solve current problems.

"In the old days, companies could only achieve this level of dialog through "game sessions" in particular towns where gamers were invited to play test games in progress in return for free sodas and snacks. Using the Internet, the same level of contact can be achieved to a far wider and more mainstream customer base."

The innovations that have emerged have helped to make GMT the leading manufacturer of its type worldwide. As a result of feedback from subscribers to the Website, for example, rules for some of the older games have been made simpler and more streamlined and the company has introduced a revolutionary new approach to historical gaming where movement and events that affect counters on a map are triggered by the skilful playing of a hand of cards – rather like a game of poker or whist – rather than by the random throw of dice. This development alone, which could not have been refined without feedback from Website subscribers, has placed GMT in an almost unassailable position in the industry.

Finally the Website has given GMT access to a new generation of young game players that they would previously have found almost impossible to target. Says MacGowan:

"An important piece of information we have gleaned from our interaction with fans on the Website is that many of them are parents, and that for many of them, playing our traditional games with their spouse and children was difficult because the games were perceived as too complicated and time-consuming."

To this end, and as a direct result of the feedback they received over the Website, MacGowan and Billingsley have launched a new division at GMT to design and produce historical games aimed at children aged 10 and upwards, games which can be played by the whole family. A typical example is *Ivanhoe: The Age of Chivalry*, in which players take on the role of a knight and use a series of cards and tokens to rally squires, gain the support of a maiden, and win tournaments.

MacGowan concludes that:

"We always wanted to tempt players back into the hobby who had played war games as teenagers and abandoned the hobby because they got married and could not carry on their hobby because it did not fit into their adult life. This latest development will, we hope, turn historical board gaming into a family activity and hopefully reach a new generation of gamers who might only have turned to computer games."

KEY LEARNING POINTS

» The "new" economy provides great opportunity for creative business opportunities, but only for those who see it as a quantum leap rather than a technological convenience.

» Businesses that use the Internet revolution to sustain or enhance the "richness" of their relationship with their customers – particularly by conducting an interactive dialog with them at every stage of a product or service's development – are those that will make this quantum leap.

» Customers are like employees. Their expectations of, for example, the level of human contact they have with the company and the services it provides are being transformed by the Internet revolution at different speeds according to the sector, their age, and their exposure to new technology. Judging the pace of speed is the key to the whole game.

The Global Dimension

Creativity has been a long time coming in terms of globalization, partly because when the whole process took off, in the wake of the Velvet Revolution in Central Europe and Deng Xiaoping's reforms in mainland China, it was throwing together business systems and cultures that were badly out of synchronization.

THEN WAS THEN AND THIS IS NOW

Western business had just undergone ten years of management revolution. Delayering and devolution of responsibility were the priorities of the age. State subsidies of business and publicly owned industries were gone or disappearing. A whole new culture was emerging, pioneered by managers who had grown up in the socially liberalized atmosphere of the 1960s and 1970s, educated in business schools that preached empowerment, teamwork, and project-based leadership.

Go back 20 years and leading corporations in both North America and Europe, as well as the social mores that shaped their cultures, would have been remarkably similar to their counterparts in other parts of the world. Religious and family values in the United States were as conservative in the 1950s as they were in China or Argentina in the 1980s. Senior managers were as parochial. State ownership, at least in Europe, was regarded as perfectly acceptable.

In the same rapid cycle of social development, the punks of Beijing and Moscow are as socially rebellious today as those in London were in the 1970s. The entrepreneurs, although they often operate more on the outer edges of commercial ethics or law, are as daring as Bill Gates or Richard Branson were in the corresponding period in the West.

So while the impact of long-established philosophies like Confucianism undoubtedly play their part – and the events following September 11, 2001 illustrate that religion is still a resurgent force in the world – it was the legacy of outdated economic systems like communism and a post-colonial trade mentality, thrown together with the doctrines of Edward E. Deming and Michael Porter, that constrained the creative potential of globalism in the early 1990s.

THE TIGERS AND THE LEASH

Asia is a good example. Despite all the talk of the tiger economies by Western commentators and Asia-Pacific industrialists, Asia set little store by innovation in the post-war era. The prosperity in almost every country was built on manufacturing existing products or delivering already established services cheaper, faster, and more efficiently.

Investors seeking out creative partners in the early wave of Western globalism had trouble finding truly innovative candidates. "We're as heavily invested in technology in Asia as any venture capital company in the world," said Bill Seymour, managing director of Singapore-based H&Q Pacific, a venture capital company part owned by the US finance house Hambrecht & Quist, as late as February 1996. "But most of the technology we see in Asia is what we call technology transfer. There's very little fundamental innovation in the companies we invest in. There's very little that is fundamentally new."

By the mid-1990s, however, all of this was changing. Asian companies were moving very fast from providing a manufacturing base for the rest of the world to being the provider of products and services for their indigenous markets. A growing breed of companies was able to collaborate with Western firms on an equal basis to develop new products for Asian consumers. Even in Communist China, the freeing up of specific economic regions from bureaucratic regulations, combined with new investment provided by the government, were helping to create startup ventures capable of entering long-term partnerships with North American or European companies to create products or services with an Asia-wide market.

Founder Group is one example of this. Set up in 1986 by Beijing University with initial seed capital of US$50,000, it now dominates the market for Chinese-language word-processing and publishing systems. By 1996, it claimed a 90 percent market share among publishing houses and news agencies in China, and a growing share of the electronic publishing market in Hong Kong, Singapore, and Malaysia.

One important reason for its success is the emphasis that company president Yan Maoxun placed on new product development. By the mid-1990s it was developing drafting instruments in partnership with Hewlett Packard and licensed patented technology developed at China's Institute of Computer Science and Technology to build a color publishing system. At the same time, the company went public on the Hong Kong Stock Exchange in order to raise funds for product research into color separation systems, multi-media, and mapping systems.

In this new climate, creativity moved fast up the priority lists of Asia's CEOs when examining the qualities they look for in their senior managers. A 1995 survey of more than 800 companies by the management journal *Asian Business* found that creativity was the attribute most wanted by Asia's recruiters – and it was also the one they perceived to be hardest to find.

The trouble was that, constrained by a paternalistic management style that emphasized obedience and conformity – one that, as we saw at the beginning of this chapter, the West had learned to discard – most Asian companies lacked the culture needed to foster and exploit genuinely creative people.

The biggest culprit, Japan, emphasized conformity, cohesion, consensus, and stability in its early campaigns to "catch up" with the West – but creativity was rarely mentioned. Inside organizations, only those who made no mistakes could succeed. Every contribution to the company was a team effort.

Management studiously avoided singling out individuals for reward or praise. A study of 700 managers in China and Japan in 1995 by the UK's Cranfield School of Management suggested that on boards and in senior management teams, senior executives felt unable to put difficult or sensitive issues on the table or criticize their superiors.

SLOGANS OR MISSIONS

For very different reasons, early attempts to foster creativity in the formerly stagnant economies of Central and Eastern Europe hit stony ground. When General Electric acquired and turned around the ailing Hungarian lighting company Tungsram in 1991, it found a workforce heavily constrained by over four decades of Communist dogma.

GE's strategy for expansion in Central and Eastern Europe was based on investment in new products, for example a range of compact fluorescent lamps that it wanted Tungsram to manufacture. A site for a dedicated plant was found at Nagykanizsa, close to the Slovenian border, where a vast manufacturing operation was built. At a cost of US$300 million it was, at the time, GE's largest single investment anywhere in the world.

In preparing Tungsram's workers for the campaign, the senior American managers for the plants encountered immediate problems in fostering the kind of creative teamwork and collaboration across different functions that was the hallmark of GE's operation in Western Europe and Northern America.

Under the socialists, exhortations to greater productivity and creativity were seen as political slogans to be ignored and bypassed. The result was that while GE executives regarded phrases such as "a culture of winning" and "empowerment" as articles of faith, to workers on the factory floor they bore a confusing similarity to the slogans of the old order.

More importantly the concept of "continuous improvement," where front-line staff have the power and discretion to make changes to ways of working, was completely alien to Central Europe at the time. GE's view was that the company should only reward measurable improvements in quality, teamwork, and initiative – but that this should be undertaken continuously. Tungsram's unions expected productivity deals to be negotiated year by year.

"Our world totally changed," says project manager Tibor Fricsan, who in 1992 saw Tungsram's layers of management cut from 11 to the current three. Tamas Palopia, senior technology director at the time, agrees: "People who are used to a hierarchical structure where the boss gave the orders had to adjust in a very short time to the idea that decisions were made by teams on the ground."

CHAOS AND CREATIVITY

In the past five years, globalism has entered a new and more turbulent phase that has encompassed Asia's stock market crash in 1998, the Seattle riots in 2000, and of course the latest crisis triggered by the terrorist attacks on the New York World Trade Center in 2001.

Many of the consequences have put the idealistic expansion of global trade, such a hallmark of the early 1990s, on a more sober footing. But, as is so often the case in times of chaos, the implications for business creativity has been largely beneficial.

For many Asian corporations, the 1998 crash was a wake-up call. A wholesale review of working procedures has been fueled by the emergence of a new generation of young workers whose perspective has not been shaped by a "salaryman" or "iron rice bowl" mentality.

The Japanese cosmetics company Shiseido is a good example. By the late 1990s, the company had notched up a series of hit products. In 1994, a new no-smudge rouge became the most successful product in the company's 123-year history. The same year Vivace Hair Fresh hair spray, designed to repel odors from the hair, produced sales of five billion units. But, in both cases, the individuals responsible were given little reward or recognition and the company continued to operate a paternalistic and insular management culture.

A series of reforms in the last four years has changed all that. In a deliberate attempt to escape the evils of hierarchy, it has abolished *sempai-kohai*, where senior managers take precedence over their junior counterparts. It has also banned the practice of addressing colleagues in the traditional fashion indicating their rank – and, in an attempt to broaden the perspective of its senior managers, encouraged them to attend internal seminars where speakers discuss topics as diverse as gymnastics and volunteer service abroad.

The breakthrough was the unexpected success of a new product, a skin lotion called *hadasiu* ("bare skin") which capitalized on Japan's boom in sales of mineral water from the slopes of Mount Fuji. Its originator, a young manager from the marketing department, in strict contrast to the past, fought senior managers head on to establish the right to lead the launch. The idea behind the launch, that skin should have mineral water to drink too, came to her, she said, after using mineral water at home in all sorts of ways. Japanese newspapers and magazines scrambled to get her story, resulting in major publicity and record sales for the product.

Siam Cement in Thailand is another example. Bunchu Pakotiprapha, manager of the company's R&D center in the early 1990s, was so desperate for staff that he resorted to advertising for external brain power over the Internet.

The difficulties Siam Cement has to contend with are remarkably similar to those faced by Japanese companies. Thailand's cultural, historical, bureaucratic, and business environment did little to encourage creativity. Thai culture is hierarchical, teaching people to obey and respect their elders. Also, the company's modern business culture is based on a trading mentality, where new breakthroughs and technology are just another part of the deal.

But with the atmosphere of head-to-head competition that has existed since the 1998 crash, where local companies have to develop their own products to maintain their standing with North American and European firms, this is no longer a situation that industry captains are prepared to tolerate.

"We need revolution, not evolution," says Dr Bancha Udomsaki, manager of Thailand's Technology Development Institute. To this end, Siam Cement is turning its R&D centers into separate companies, with the autonomy to set their own salaries and perks, allowing managers to reward individuality and creativity – a practice boosted by the fact that Thai companies can now deduct one and a half times the actual R&D expenses from their taxable income.

DIVERSITY AND DIASPORA

Western companies have also changed. As is explained in more depth in the counterpart chapter to this one in the ExpressExec title *The Innovative Individual*, they have moved from imposing their own conformity on overseas subsidiaries or offices to deliberately tapping the diversity of local staff.

As early as 1994, a survey on expatriate management in Asia by the Economist Intelligence Unit indicated that the leading reason companies were moving staff around the region was to form multi-cultural project teams. But at the time, this was largely to brief the parent company on local conditions and to act as "gatekeepers." Now, as *The Innovative Individual* highlights, it is to develop truly international products or services.

Western employers are able to do this at home as well as abroad, because inter-community movement has (subject to any crackdown on immigration that might occur as a result of the events of September 11, 2001) strengthened the diaspora that have often been a powerhouse of innovation around the world, most notable the overseas and largely Cantonese diaspora that have spread to Australasia and North America and the Bengali and Punjabi diaspora that have spread to East Africa and the UK.

This has generated a new set of second- or third-generation young-sters that are keen to work for large organizations, either to escape from or to prepare themselves for working in their parents' family firms, but who still have a diverse or different view of the markets their employers target.

From a creative agenda, it does matter what culture helped to shape this perspective. Michael Eisner, the man who turned around the Disney corporation in the 1980s, argues that much of the recent vitality of the company comes from the fact that his creative teams are recruited from the rich mix of cultures that now make up California's population. In a recent interview for *Harvard Business Review*, he states:

> "I'm not just talking about diversity in skin color or ethnic background, I'm talking about diversity as a point of view. We want people who work here to look at the world differently from each other. They can be white, they can be Indian or Chinese or Latino – it does not really matter. The important thing is that they can look at the same problem and bring their own individuality to the solution."

And this, more than any other benefit, is the real creative payback of globalism. When the process started, the cultural divides of parent companies and the host countries from which local staff would be recruited were clearly visible. Whether it was a Japanese automotive company setting up in Wales or an American lighting company setting up in Hungary, the technology and knowledge transfer was one-way and top-down.

Spain's Banco de Bilbao y Viscaya (BBV), when it expanded into Latin America in the mid-1990s, developed a "hit squad" of 100 experts in areas such as IT, marketing, human resources, retail banking, and financial operations. Reporting directly to the chief executive in Madrid, five or six of this group were sent into every bank that BBV acquired to create a management structure similar to that the bank had developed at home.

Interviewed in the business magazine *MBA* in 1998, BBV's chief executive José Igancio Goirigolzarri commented:

> "When we buy into a Latin American bank and obtain a management agreement, we first of all carry out a thorough restructuring exercise. The main objectives are to improve efficiency and profitability, and to fit the acquisition into the BBV mold. For example,

BBV's IT system is installed in each Latin American bank that is brought by the BBV network.

"We are now bringing over to Spain from Latin America key top local managers of the future for our Latin American operations. They then spend two or three years working with BBV in Spain, and we also arrange for them to bring their families over with them. This is a very large operation but it is essential in order to give the managers the necessary feel for the BBV way of doing things."

"Our way of doing things" and "fitting acquisitions into the mold" is a pretty good summary of what international companies tried to instil in the early years of globalism. Now things, and people, are on the move. The diaspora linking home communities in developing countries to the richer countries of North America and Western Europe is stronger and now encompasses not just Cantonese and Bengalis but newer economic migrants such as Afghans, Vietnamese, Russians, Uzbeks, and Nepalese.

This in turn is creating a richer mix of perspectives and insights on which organizations can draw, either when they are recruiting their own staff or when looking for partners and suppliers. Eisner's concept of diversity as a creative force rather than just an ethical point of principle is catching on. "Diversity is about individuals," says Susan Lax, diversity manager for McDonald's in the UK. "By valuing different life experiences, different backgrounds and different ideas, we believe companies like ours will reap the rewards in wholly new perspectives on our markets, customers and future growth."

CASE STUDY: NOON PRODUCTS

Britain's Punjabi and Bengali communities are proving the same creative force in the UK that the overseas Chinese and Latino diaspora are in California and the Gulf. Well-established experts in active business partnering, they are looking for UK collaborators to break into new markets to take advantage of the UK's growing presence in European markets, offering in return the financial and trading acumen of an Asian diaspora which stretches from Cape Town to Bombay and Hong Kong.

Walk into any of a number of specific UK supermarkets, like Sainsbury and Waitrose. Buy any of the wide range of ready-prepared Indian and Chinese meals from the chill box and the chances are that it will have been prepared by Noon Products, a decade-old business that by the late 1990s was achieving an annual turnover of over £30mn.

The biography of Noon Products' founder, Gulam Khaderboy Noon, since his arrival in Britain is fairly typical of first-generation Asians who have settled in the UK during the last 30 years. Born in Bombay in 1936, his family had been in business since 1898, when his grandfather opened up a Bombay confectionery shop.

Noon inherited the business from his father when he was 17 and brought his expertise to Britain in 1971. His timing was impeccable. A large part of the east-African Asian diaspora had just settled in the UK following persecution in Kenya and Uganda, and there was a sudden demand for Indian sweets and savories.

Supported by a UK-based partner, the British Asian Company, he set up Bombay Halwa Sweets and the brand name for one of his products, "Bombay Mix," has now become almost as generic a term for Indian confectionery as "Hoover" once was for vacuum cleaners.

Dissatisfied with the scope for expansion in a highly confined market, Noon looked elsewhere for sources of growth. The influx of the east-African communities also brought a boost in popularity for more authentic Indian food among the indigenous British – many of whose tastes had been shaped by the fad for frozen curries among students and flat-dwellers in the early 1970s.

The problem was that these early versions of Indian food were god-awful. "The demand was there but the food in the freezers was dreadful," Noon comments. "It was insipid, tasteless and badly packaged. Nobody had really worked out how to mass-manufacture Indian food while retaining its real flavor. I decided to find a way."

Technology and the advent of chilled foods in the supermarket unlocked the solution. In 1980, Noon went to the US for four years and joined the Taj hotel and catering group, where he researched the technology needed to manufacture Indian food on a grand scale. In 1987, he set up Noon Products and persuaded first Bird's Eye and then Waitrose and Sainsbury to buy his products.

The key to Noon's success was his insistence that there should be no trade-off between technological mass-manufacturing techniques and the authenticity of the finished product. Chefs at Noon Products take up to six months to develop each recipe and longer if the client wants a full range, as happened in 1996 with Waitrose when there was a sudden surge in demand for Goan cooking. "What instantly attracted Noon to us was that he used the best processes and methods but never at the expense of quality," says Bob Cooper, the director at Sainsbury that founded the partnership.

In the early days of the business, when little appropriate technology existed for what he wanted to achieve, Noon worked closely with specialist engineering companies in the US and Europe to develop or adapt the right machinery. When he started the company, for instance, there was a great fad for *tikka* – marinated and baked chicken or lamb – in UK restaurants but no means to mass-manufacture it. Noon tracked down and adapted a machine in Germany used to prepare *charcuterie* for Bavarian supermarkets which had the right "rolling mechanism" to properly marinade the meat before it was oven-baked.

"I am not an engineer by profession but I have an open and inquiring mind about food technology," he says. "If someone has a machine that will help me, I will travel the world to seek it out."

Because he has an open and inquiring mind, Noon picks up inspiration from anywhere. Born into a country with the largest film industry in the world – Bombay is nicknamed "Bollywood" – Noon has been an avid film buff since childhood, and finds time to go to the cinema nearly every week.

He is inspired and draws lessons from the pyrotechnics of Hollywood blockbuster directors like Stephen Spielberg, James Cameron, and Ridley Scott. "The effects they achieve in films like *Titanic* or *Jurassic Park* fascinate me," he says. "I want to jump up and stop the movie mid-stream to find out how they achieve them. I come away thinking that if they can push out the boundaries of what technology can achieve in their industry, I can in mine."

KEY LEARNING POINTS

» The contrast between the cultures of Western companies and those from other regions may not be so deep-seated as was first thought. Creativity is becoming a global priority.

» This is being helped along by two by-products of global free trade. The first is that Western companies are moving from imposing conformity of overseas subsidiaries and division towards tapping the diversity of perspectives their staff contribute to product development and strategic decision-making; the second is that greater freedom of movement is leading to economic migrants strengthening the diaspora of particular races or communities, which are in turn enriching the local labor markets of the developed world.

Creativity: The State of the Art

Two aspects of creativity dominate in the modern corporation. The first is the relationship between the organization and the individual and how the way a person thinks, feels about, and sees the firm impacts on his or her creative capability. This is the subject of a separate ExpressExec title: *The Innovative Individual*.

The second aspect, which will be dealt with in detail in this chapter, is how people collectively interact with each other to spark, shape, and test ideas. As Chapter 2 highlighted, creativity in business is a collective process. The rise in importance of innovation during the 1990s coincided with the team and the project as the source of all change and energy.

But whereas teamwork and project management at the start of the decade were founded on the methods and culture of the engineering and construction industries – where critical path analysis and cost control reign supreme – team co-ordinators and project leaders now take their inspiration from sectors where ideas rather than artifacts are the main outputs.

The role they play is very different, as are the methods used.

TURNING UP THE HEAT

Anthony Jay, the former BBC producer and founder of the cutting-edge video training company Video Arts, once described the output of creative groups in this way:

> "Output is necessary in the first instance as a spur to ideas: the knowledge that a deadline is approaching, that something has to be done urgently, is a wonderful liberator of the creative impulse. That is why the 'wastage' principle does not work with creative groups. The idea of getting ten groups all to put in an idea from which one will be selected and nine discarded does not get the best out of these groups: the sense of urgency is divided by ten. It is much better, very often, for the one group to bear the responsibility alone, to know that every-thing depends on what they are coming up with, and that good or bad it will go into production because there is nothing else."

Jay's description highlights the first priority in any collective creative work. The participants have to be intellectually engaged and they will only be so if they feel the work of the group places them on the line.

"Creativity and adaptation are born of tension, passion, and conflict," says Californian guru Richard Pascale. "Contention does more than make us creative. It makes us whole, it propels us along the journey of development."

The sense of it is what matters. Sometimes the work of the group is so obviously linked to a matter of life or death that nobody needs to be told. The crisis management team that managed the benzene contamination crisis at Perrier in 1987 knew perfectly well that the survival of the company depended on what they did. The Board did not need to say it. A glance at the morning papers or the evening news bulletin told them all they needed to know.

In most cases, this "sense" needs to be created. Team members will only acquire the interactive tension they need to do their best work if they are persuaded that it is linked to the organization's key goals. Indeed there are those, like Richard Pascale and Ronald Heifetz of the John F. Kennedy School of Government (see Chapter 8), that argue that "framing" the work of key teams and projects in this way is the principal and overriding role of every chief executive.

Heifetz likens the role to that of regulating a pressure cooker. Someone – it could be the organization's chief executive or the team's own leader – needs to turn up the heat while simultaneously allowing some of the steam to escape. If the pressure exceeds the cooker's capacity, the cooker can blow up. However, nothing cooks without some heat.

A good example of an organization without any heat at all was the UK's sole meal-ticket company in the mid-1980s, Luncheon Vouchers. Precisely because it lacked a domestic competitor – the tax allowances of the day did not offer much of a margin to commercial suppliers – the company was staid, lacking in energy, and complacent.

In 1986, the inevitable occurred. The company was taken over by the French hotel and catering giant Accor. The new chief executive, Olivier de Bosredon, immediately set about looking for ways to put the staff on their mettle when there was no good reason on their home turf for them to make the effort.

Part of the task was accomplished by linking the company's targets and future resources to Accor's meal-ticket business in other countries – which was currently undergoing a period of rapid expansion, particularly in Latin America. The major leap forward, however, was a company-wide exercise pitting each department against a counterpart in a fictitious competitor in the UK.

Exercises like this can fall flat on their face because they are perceived by participants as so patently cosmetic. But de Bosredon put a great deal of effort into the design, turning the exercise into a giant think tank. The scenarios and targets given to each work unit exposed the vulnerability of the company to overseas competition, set Luncheon Vouchers effectively in the context of the British catering industry, and provided a series of intellectually stimulating challenges.

Run over a two-week period, the various departments were invited to match or exceed performance targets of the fictitious competitor set by de Bosredon and the company's sales and marketing director Sue Harvey. Both departmental and individual prizes were offered to the winners and a collective goal was set to all staff to put the competitor out of business by exceeding all the pre-set performance goals.

An internal newsletter to provide daily bulletins of the battle between the companies was set up, culminating in a full-page front cover article announcing the demise of the competitor when, much to the delight of de Bosredon and Harvey, the targets were all reached or exceeded.

What de Bosredon achieved with what might have been dismissed as a minor training exercise was to get the company collectively to think about its future. In the short-term, customer complaints were slashed to one-fifth of their previous level through the energy created by the exercise.

The long-term benefits were felt throughout the whole of the following decade. Harvey took over as managing director and, profiting from ideas generated by the exercise, she pushed the company outside the narrow constraints of its original sector, developing voucher schemes for both childcare and healthcare and laying the foundations for the organization's present role as a leading provider of employee assistance programs.

Pushing the heat up too far can prove destructive. Michael Eisner's abrasive management style, deliberately pitting one executive against another, has resulted in Disney losing some of its best creative animators. To come up with the layout for Disneyland Paris (formerly EuroDisney) he called a meeting of a dozen of the world's most respected architects and had them brainstorm in a widely abrasive session that became so heated, two of the architects began shoving each other and almost came to blows.

However, advocates of creative tension point out that too often the opposite of conflict is apathy. Dorothy Leonard, a professor at Harvard Business School and the author of *Where Sparks Fly*, puts it this way. Managers who dislike conflict – or value only their own approach – actively avoid a clash of ideas.

They hire and reward people of a particular type, usually people like themselves. Their organization then becomes victim of what Leonard calls "comfortable clone syndrome." Co-workers share similar interests and training, and everyone thinks alike. Because ideas all pass through similar cognitive filters, only familiar ones survive.

A manager successful at fostering innovation, Leonard argues, values people with a variety of thinking styles and figures out how to get them to grate against each other in a process she calls "creative abrasion." Such a manager understands that different people have different styles: analytical or intuitive, conceptual or experimental, social or independent, logical or values-driven. He or she sets the ground rules for how people work together.

TEAM LEADER: SWORD AND SHIELD

All of this places a great deal of pressure on the team manager or project leader. Commentators like Leonard and Anthony Jay (see above) see these people as the pivot of the creative process.

"If a creative leader is removed from a group, it becomes an extinct volcano," says Jay. "If a firm wants to weaken a competitor, one of the cheapest and most effective ways is to identify the creative groups and offer the leaders lucrative and attractive jobs on its own staff. It is not important that it should need them itself, although they ought to prove an invaluable addition to the strength, only that the competitor should be deprived of them."

Why is this? Because, as Leonard stresses, team leaders in a project-based organization have direct control over almost everything that will determine whether the output is genuinely creative or a damp squib.

They influence or appoint who is on the team, drawing on their memory to select the right balance of lateral thinkers, specialists, and shapers – often plucking out people who have been sidelined in their careers and have something to prove. They protect "loners," ensuring that their lack of team or social skills does not result in their contribution being dismissed or marginalized. They shield the team from the unrealistic expectations of the Board or broader organization, negotiating the time and the resources it needs to fulfill its remit.

Above all, they determine the way the group works. As the remit of teams has moved from finding the best way of fulfilling a pre-ordained task to generating original ideas of their own, a great deal of constructive attention has been focused on the way ideas are inspired and shaped collectively – and traditional methods have been found wanting.

"The trouble with brainstorming is that everybody thinks they already do it," says Tom Kelly of the US design giant IDEO. "Their eyes glaze over when I mention that brainstorming is an art, more like playing the piano than tying your shoes, because they equate brainstorming as being no more than an animated meeting."

Kelly's criticisms of brainstorming as it is often conducted in meetings are very similar to those made by psychologists during the past three decades, including Alex Osborn, Edward de Bono, and Tudor Rickards (see Chapter 8). Black-and-white thinking shuts out wild ideas that, while they might be unworkable, get participants to think "out of their box."

The tendency for both the originators of ideas and their critics to analyze any new suggestion to death before it is barely out of the mouth cuts off the flow of original thought. There is nearly always a lack of understanding among participants and organizers that what counts in a brainstorm is not the quality of ideas but their volume – because the energy this creates moves peoples' thinking forward. There is often no sense of play, no sense of fun, and no sense of ease.

Kelly's own company, founded by his brother David in 1978 and based in California, has been responsible for a stunningly diverse range of products, from the Polaroid I-Zone camera to Crest Toothpaste's Neat Squeeze tube.

At IDEO, brainstorming "the right way" is used as the principal means of tapping collective thought. Design teams are expected to make mistakes early and often. Coming to the right solution too quickly is discouraged. People are encouraged to question any and all assumptions and are not regarded as innovative unless they are challenging the client's, the team's, and their own pre-existing notions.

Conference rooms have brainstorming rules stenciled on the walls in six-inch letters, including "Encourage wild ideas" and "Be visual." Rather than using the emerging digital technologies for group work to collect ideas, low-tech tools like markers, giant Post-It Notes, and rolls of paper on tables are used to better effect.

Sketching, diagrams, mind-mapping, and primitive visual imagery like stick figures enable facilitators to capture the ideas because they keep pace with the energy of the discussion and are physical. The basic traps of brainstorming are avoided such as letting the boss go first (he or she will set the agenda and boundaries, immediately limiting the brainstorm), taking turns (democratic, painless, and pointless, according to Kelly), and relying on the contribution of experts who may have the right knowledge but not the perspective or insight to see beyond it.

Building on the work of team discussions are contributions from an array of players who have an equal role to play in turning an idea into a fully-blown commercial proposition. As we highlighted in Chapter 2, our own research suggests that over and above the people directly involved in shaping breakthroughs in thinking or insight, a number of other equally important roles need to be in place.

These include "sponsors," the people who promote the idea inside the organization, ensuring that it is not dismissed at birth and sustaining interest in it during the prolonged period of gestation. They include "sounding boards," people outside the project whose objectivity and broader knowledge of the field can be drawn on to inform or validate the premise or to comment on the practicalities. And they include "specialists," people who draw on expert knowledge or skills to shape the idea from a specific standpoint, often using the opportunity to break new ground in their own field.

These roles are often best played by managers or specialists who are external to the organization or on the periphery, because their position enables them to step back and frame the concept or idea in a broader canvas.

The design and construction of British Airways' Waterside headquarters near Heathrow Airport, which used pioneering architecture and workspace design to promote new ways of working, was "informed" by a number of well-placed external experts. The concept of using communal social facilities to promote serendipity and cross-functional working was influenced by the work of two academics at the University of London's Bartlett School of Architecture, Dr Tadeusz Grajewski and Professor Bill Hillier, in a report entitled *The Social Potential of Buildings*. The creation of "club" working, BA's version of hot-desking, was designed and overseen by an architectural consultant, Kathy Tilney. The expertise required to wire the building in a way that would allow staff access to their database and messages anywhere inside or outside the building was supplied by R&D staff working for BA's principal telecomm suppliers.

It was the renaissance perspective of these individuals rather than just their expert knowledge that made them valuable to BA. Kathy Tilney, for example, has a long-standing interest in the relationship between people and buildings which is fueled by a secret childhood ambition to be an anthropologist. She is particularly fascinated by how ancient civilizations on different sides of the world with no apparent contact developed similar customs, myths, and ceremonies – and it is not difficult to see how this private interest feeds into work trying to fathom the complexities of human interaction in large corporations.

CHOOSING THE WINNING IDEA

Once the product of this intellectual endeavor has reached a certain point, the corporation will have to decide whether to back it to the hilt or write it off as a useful but over-risky pilot.

The survival of pharmaceutical companies, for example, depends almost entirely on the internal investment decisions made by its senior managers regarding which research projects to favor and which to abandon.

GlaxoSmithKline claims that its ability to sustain a steady stream of new products is the result not just of luck and largesse but also of swiftly killing projects that seem unlikely to yield results and searching for new uses of old drugs. (For example, Lamivudine, a new treatment for hepatitis launched in 1996, is essentially a lower-dose version of 3TC, one of the firm's AIDS drugs.)

Its effectiveness in making these decisions was boosted in the early 1990s by reforms introduced by an impromptu partnership of managers working for SmithKline Beecham (as it was then), Paul Sharpe, director of project management in neuroscience at the company's Harlow (UK) plant, and Tom Keelin of the Strategic Decisions Group, an international management consulting firm based in Menlo Park, California.

Sharpe and Keelin reviewed the way in which investment decisions about seed-corn R&D projects were made, and they did not like what they found. In come cases, decisions to favor one project over another were made by little more than a show of hands. In other cases, projects were scored using seemingly objective criteria like commercial potential, technical risk, and investment requirements. But the information underpinning these criteria was provided almost entirely by project champions who stood to win or lose by all the decisions, since little attempt was made to draw any lessons or useful insights from projects that were terminated.

To increase more transparency into the process, the two managers developed a new decision-making framework. Each project team competing for investment had to brainstorm, under controlled conditions, how they would respond in the case of four different outcomes. These were that:

» They won the funding they were looking for;
» They won less funding;
» They won more funding; or
» They won no funding but were asked to salvage what they could from what they had already achieved.

The benefits the company gained from this new approach were significant. First, it got teams to start their discussions from the standpoint that this was not a win-all/lose-all situation. Projects that would have been eliminated under the previous all-or-nothing approach were given a chance of survival. Project champions were also less inclined to exaggerate or distort the claims or statistics on which the decision would be made.

Second, the cross-team synergy that resulted from the brainstorming created a fresh pool of ideas that would otherwise have been lost and that were often applicable to other projects. The requirement for the team to consider what aspects of their project could be salvaged in the event of a failed bid resulted in a win-win situation because the losers gained as much credit for their work as the winners.

Identifying which business ideas have real commercial value is one of the most difficult challenges faced by any organization. Not unsurprisingly, a number of business school academics have developed models that they can use to invest their resources wisely.

The now celebrated partnership of W. Chan Kim and Renée Mauborgne at Insead in Fontainebleau has developed six "utility levers" to test the market viability of new ideas:

» *Customer productivity*: What is the biggest block to customer productivity? How does the innovative product or service eliminate it? Example: Dyson's bagless vacuum cleaner made the job quicker and easier.
» *Simplicity*: What is the greatest source of complexity for all customers? How does the innovation dramatically simplify this? Example: Intuit's *Quicken* software eliminates accountancy jargon.
» *Convenience*: What is the greatest inconvenience for customers? How does the innovation remove it? Example: Virgin's limousine service for business class travelers helped ease the hassle of getting to and from the airport.
» *Risk*: What are the greatest uncertainties customers face? How does the innovation eliminate these risks? Example: The utility company Enron took the volatility out of gas prices with its commodity swaps and futures contracts.
» *Fun and image*: What are the biggest blocks to fun and image? How does the innovation add emotion or cachet? Example: Starbucks coffee bars offer more than simply a place to drink coffee.
» *Environmental friendliness*: What causes the greatest harm to the environment? How does the innovation reduce or eliminate this?

Example: Phillips' Alto lightbulb, using less mercury, allowed fluorescent office lighting to be disposed of without special dumps.

Kim and Mauborgne also stress that taking the right decision about who to partner with is critical to the successful exploitation of any new concept or idea. Many innovators try to carry out all the production and distribution themselves, they argue, with disastrous results. No one organization has all the capabilities they need and unless the resulting product is extremely well protected in terms of either patenting or intellectual copyright, time works against the innovator in favor of the imitator.

MIND GAMES

Whether the creativity lies in the day-to-day innovations that transform the way the organization works or the strategic decisions that determine where the firm should invest its resources, senior managers are becoming acutely aware that how individuals or teams *see* their work is as important as the skills and knowledge at their disposal.

Analyzing the value of science and history to the business world, the distinguished Oxford biologist Richard Dawkins recently wrote that their study did not provide managers with transferable solutions but the opportunity to see common or emerging problems from a different perspective.

In brainstorms, it has long been commonplace for groups to "get a new take" on the challenge in hand using analogy and metaphor. A tried and tested exercise is to use a metaphor describing the challenge or situation, such as "without the right marketing strategy we will be like a bird of prey with a squint" as a starting point for discussion. The concept builds on the premise that our use of language shapes the way we look on the world.

Professor Johan Roos of the International Institute for Management Development (IMD) in Lausanne takes the importance of language and perspective a stage further. He sees organizations as little more than "systems of language." As he comments:

"Managers need to pay more attention to the language that is used in organizations. The use of language differs among many levels and groups. How and why members of the organization choose particular words in communicating with others is critical. The choice of words provides an intellectual and emotional context for the way in which subordinates and colleagues relate to, and make sense of, their work. This in turn has an important influence on their performance.''

Roos argues that the language used in most organizations is unique to it and, because it shapes the outlook of its workforce, is directly related to the way it innovates and responds to change. If the language is alive and vibrant, responding to the influx of new ideas and people, the outlook it helps to shape will keep the organization alive to the events around it. If it is stultified, jargon-ridden, and shaped only by senior executives, so too will be the culture.

The force for change, in terms of both language and culture, will nearly always come from the outside. Our own research on how ideas are shaped (see Chapter 8) suggests that the overwhelming majority of ideas (90% plus) are triggered outside the workplace and inspired by a range of activities that include personal and professional networking, conference presentations, private or professional study, private or professional reading, sport or other leisure activities, community work, or family life.

Sport, for example, is an immensely popular source of inspiration in professional life. On a day-to-day level it influences both the techniques and management style used in the workplace, in terms of teamwork, coaching, and motivation. P.Y. Gerbeau, the charismatic manager who attempted with mixed success to turn around London's Millennium Dome, drew heavily on the insights and experience gained from an earlier career as a professional hockey player and coach.

On a more fundamental level, sport has replaced the post-war reliance on military metaphor and analogy as the biggest shaper of business language and perspective. Work we undertook for the UK Institute of Personnel and Development on the people aspects of lean production in the early 1990s, for example, suggests that how an organization determines the main thrust of its HR strategy depends, in part, on what messages its senior managers derive from sporting metaphors and analogies. The terms "lean" and "fit" are both sporting metaphors but whereas leanness suggests that workers are merely fat for the shedding, fitness suggests they form part of a muscular and cardiovascular infrastructure that needs building up through systematic development.

In an effort to shape how its key workers see the organization and the challenges it confronts, senior managers and business schools have extended the remit of executive courses to expose participants to new thinking, not only inspired by the latest management theories but by concepts in other fields.

In Japan, to broaden their perspective, senior managers at Shiseido, a cosmetics company, attend seminars where speakers discuss topics as diverse as gymnastics and Japan's volunteer medical service in developing countries. In the UK, the Cranfield School of Management has linked up with the Globe Theatre to launch the Praxis Centre, which offers a series of programs in which current management issues are discussed in the context of Shakespeare's plays.

In Italy, Alfredo Ambrosetti, a leading consultant, runs Alpha Plus, a learning club for chief executives and board directors who pay an annual subscription to attend monthly meetings led by leading thinkers, politicians, philosophers, and journalists. Similarly, in France, Henri-Claude de Bettignes oversees the AVIRA program, where 15 senior executives selected by de Bettignes meet to debate matters of mutual concern in Singapore, California, or at Insead's Fontainebleau campus. A topic at one meeting was "Can humanists run companies?"

CREATIVITY IN A RECESSION

In Chapter 1, we argued that recessions were the time when creative thinking was most needed but often least available. How can organizations hold onto the creative resources they need when they are almost inevitably required to make job cuts and promotion freezes that will demotivate their workforce?

The first way forward is to take measures to ensure that they do not completely lose their "corporate memory" when they make necessary staff cuts. In part this can be done by using the more sophisticated technology at their disposal to record how breakthroughs in products, services, and ways of working in recent years were achieved in practice.

The focus should be not simply on keeping a record of what was achieved but rather on the thinking behind it. Rather like scientists record every stage of an experiment as it occurs so that they or their successors can "backtrack" to trace the creative chain, so project leaders and team leaders can record how they reached key decisions, so that once they move on the "guardians" of the innovation during bad times do not lose touch with the spirit that prompted it.

At 3M, one of the world's most innovative companies, great care goes into the language used in recording experiments and product development projects. Bullet-point summaries are banned and writers are encouraged to use a narrative style that captures the excitement and lateral-minded spirit that motivated team members and supplier-client partnerships. "Maybe our story-intensive culture is just an accident but we don't think so," says Gordon Shaw, the executive director who pioneered the changes. "We sense that it is part of the way we see ourselves and explain ourselves to one another and to the people who will join us in the future."

The second way of preserving the organization's corporate memory is by recognizing that the people who are axed do not vaporize into thin air. In a recession, they are less likely to join a competitor. If the exit is handled sensitively, it may be possible to buy them back into the company on a flexible as and when basis to bring their successors back up to stream with their thinking about past innovations and future implications.

Research by the charity New Ways to Work, which champions flexible working, has shown how imaginative use of part-time and contract working can bring benefits in creative thought as well as cost efficiencies. As one of two job sharers profiled in their latest report *Flexi-Exec* comments: "I can talk to someone who is as involved in the subject as I am and who shares my interest in finding the best solution."

In addition, there are ways in which organizations can keep in touch with events on the ground, to keep them thinking beyond the present. While cuts in training and the use of consultants or external advisers may be necessary, a total freeze on all development activity could blinker the collective perspective of the firm. Encouraging staff to attend conferences and industry fora and then report back their findings on new developments will yield significant benefits. This can be undertaken systematically through think tanks, benchmarking exercises, and syndicate discussion groups, all supported by company intranets and discussional databases.

KEY LEARNING POINTS

» The style in which creative teamwork is undertaken is critical to its success. Free thinking, freedom from censure, and creative abrasion are some of the many common features.

» For this reason, the role of the team leader or project manager is pivotal. He or she will usually choose members of the group and determine the working style. Team leaders also act as the "shield" for the team, protecting it from the unrealistic expectations of the external organization, and the "resource gatherer," negotiating it the means it needs to get the job done.

» Imaginative assessment techniques will be needed to judge which creative output from a variety of teams is worth backing and which needs to be abandoned. If possible, this system of assessment should ensure that the thinking and insights of projects deemed to be "failures" are nonetheless preserved and transferred.

» Creative thinking is as important to an organization's survival during a recession as it is during a boom. Firms should find new ways to capture the creative thinking that helped shaped recent innovations, preserve their "corporate memory," and find the resources to enable their staff to keep in touch with current developments and report these back.

Creativity in Practice:

Four Case Studies

» British Airways: the pivotal role of the team leader
» BMW: fostering experimentation in the assembly line
» Spearhead China: managing a creative exchange
» Nortel Networks: fostering innovation in the front line

BRITISH AIRWAYS: THE PIVOTAL ROLE OF THE TEAM LEADER

In Chapter 6, we looked at the importance of the role played by team leaders in determining the success of any creative project, not only because they usually select the members of the team and negotiate the time, space, and resources it needs, but because they determine how it works.

In 1998, British Airways relocated 3500 staff to a new purpose-built headquarters, Waterside, on the perimeter of London's Heathrow Airport. What made this initiative exceptional was the link BA made between the design of the building and its internal workspace and the creative output of its workers (see Chapter 2).

Waterside was the brainchild of the general manager of Property in the late 1980s, Gwliym Rees-Jones, who – inspired by the work of the Bartlett School of Architecture (see Chapter 6) – worked closely with Norwegian architect and former town planner Neils Torp to ensure that the building fostered serendipity and creative interchanges between staff from different departments, thus eliminating the turf wars that had plagued the company in the run up to its privatization in 1987.

Torp, under Rees-Jones's guidance, came up with a design in which six self-contained buildings are linked by "The Street," a corporate boulevard with its own shops, restaurants, and cafes. Rees-Jones envisaged that BA would be able to use this facility to establish a "no office culture" where staff would be encouraged to hold most of their meetings in The Street rather than in their own workspace. This throughput of people from different parts of the building, coupled with visitors and BA staff from other sites, would result in the serendipity he wished to achieve.

In 1991, having won the backing of the Board, Rees-Jones was transferred to another project. The responsibility for ensuring that his vision for the building was made real devolved onto a project development team headed by a former colleague, Chris Byron.

Almost as soon as he took over, Byron realized that the creative "touchy feely" side of the project, in a classic macho construction environment, was in danger of being sacrificed to the short-term needs of getting the building up and running by its target date of October 1998.

To forestall this Byron took a number of steps:

» When selecting the project team, he chose people who either had a background in organizational behavior or understood the links between workspace design and productivity. The facilities manager, for example, was chosen because she had recently taken a Masters degree that focused on human behavior at work and was keen to put the concepts she had learned into practice.

» He capped, early on, the proportion of the total budget that could be spent on the external building, to prevent the cost of construction eating into money earmarked for the design of the offices and "The Street."

» Also early on in the project, he commissioned a report from design consultants Tilney Shane that spelt out the likely needs of users based on a survey of the staff that were going to be transferred.

» He used the findings of this report, and Rees-Jones's original vision for Waterside, to resolve any disputes. "Whenever someone pushed out the boat too far for other people's comfort, I would place the vision in front of them and ask whether their proposal would further its aims," he says. "If they could make the link, it was actively considered. If they couldn't, it was thrown out."

Byron's relationship with other team members was the key to the success of the project. Because he had not opted for the most obvious high flyers but rather people whose enthusiasm was based on intellectual engagement rather than corporate ladder-climbing, their was little homogeneity in their working style.

His leadership style needed to reflect this. It was on-site – as soon as progress permitted, the team worked from Portakabins adjacent to the building – and very inclusive. Every member of the team was given the opportunity and – equally important – the time to make their contribution to any point of dispute. As Byron recalls:

"We did not work to a rigid time-scale. I did not try to drive things through like a professional chairman because railroading of this kind results in a lack of consensus that jumps back at you further down the line. There were too many people with too many strong views and vested interests. Consequently I adopted a more facilitating style, giving everyone five minutes to stress what issues they felt were at stake.

"Of course everyone took more time – up to 15 minutes in some cases – but I was prepared to let the discussion go on if it helped to enrich our collective perspective. Obviously I had to pull things together and make a decision. But taking the time and patience to listen to the issues, sometimes for longer than you really want to, helps create a common language in a team made up from different backgrounds and disciplines."

This emphasis on consensus paid off. All the members of the team are united in stressing that Byron's leadership style was critical not only in getting the project completed on-time and on-budget but in fully tapping everyone's creative potential. Says facilities manager Alison Hartigan:

"Over a period of time I became best buddies with people who were to me like chalk and cheese. The respect for each other's knowledge – built up because Chris gave us the space and time we needed to acquire it – resulted in collective insights during our brainstorms that seem to come from nowhere. Even where there were disputes, Chris was incredibly good at problem-solving. You were given the confidence to throw anything you liked at him. You never had to preface your remarks by asking whether it was a dumb question. You threw anything you liked into the ring."

BMW: FOSTERING EXPERIMENTATION IN THE ASSEMBLY LINE

In Chapter 6, we saw how important it is for managers to send out the right signals to their staff if they want to encourage the kind of experimentation that leads to breakthroughs in product or service development or new ways of working. If people are penalized for taking risks that fail, no amount of rhetoric will counteract the damage.

A further constraint is the financial cost of experimentation, real or perceived. In manufacturing, for example, early prototypes require a new set of tools: equipment which is expensive to manufacture and which is usually scrapped if the experiment is abandoned. The perception of cost in the mind of research and technical staff causes them to rein back their wild ideas and only undertake serious prototype work on projects with a serious prospect of success. In this way they close down mental avenues that might lead to unexpected or unpredictable breakthroughs.

The German luxury car manufacturer BMW addressed this problem in the mid-1990s by developing a new way to manufacture prototype parts, which cut the cost to a fraction of what it was before. Laser modeling allows the company's staff to mold reinforced plastic into parts that would enable them to undertake initial prototype work with metal parts only when the first trials had been undertaken successfully.

The "trial and error" learning approach was furthered at the R&D center in Munich by having a fully operational car assembly line on the ground floor, capable of producing more than 3000 cars a year. As Hans Honig, manager of welding and joining systems, explains:

> "This acts as a live 'testing ground,' enabling designers to check how and in what conditions the parts they have designed are fitted on the assembly line, hand-in-hand with members of staff who are being trained to oversee the future production of any new series. Because production methods and procedures are tested in realistic conditions, problems can be identified and dealt with at an early stage, so that the start of production in other plants is much smoother."

SPEARHEAD CHINA: MANAGING A CREATIVE EXCHANGE

Also in Chapter 6, we highlight the findings of research by Harvard Business School's Dorothy Leonard that members of creative groups need to be selected for their different deep knowledge as well as different culture and thinking styles, to provide the right intellectual diversity.

Grand Metropolitan (GrandMet), prior to the merger with Guinness in 1996 that created the corporation now known as Diagio, was in the middle of transforming itself from an assortment of subsidiaries in industries as disparate as hotels and eyecare to an integrated group of companies focusing solely on branded food and drink products.

This coincided with the opening up of new economic opportunities in developing countries in the wake of the collapse of Communism. GrandMet's chief executive in 1994, George Bull, made the exploitation of new markets in India, Russia, and China a driving force for closer creative collaboration between firms that had previously been linked only by common financial ownership.

This was not easy to achieve. A world separated the traditions of American companies in the GrandMet group like Pilsbury, Burger King, and Häagen Dazs from those of UK counterparts like the ITT Group, which controlled top drinks brands like Smirnoff and J&B. All these companies had previously pursued their own strategies in developing economies and there was about as much willingness to exchange vital data and insights with executives from sister companies in the corporation as there was to do so with competitors.

The Group HR department recognized this and proposed a series of workshops for senior managers from across GrandMet that would provide a forum for discussion and expert insight on the practicalities of doing business in the key economies of Asia and Eastern Europe. The issues would be raised and explored by expert consultants, practitioners and consultants but the purpose of the exercise was not for participants to soak up specialist information that they might already have access to in their own companies but to provoke a creative interchange between each other. Up-front research by the HR department revealed that some executives had up to 20 years of experience in the economies under scrutiny while others were novices. In this sense, the workshops would be classic exercises in organizational learning.

The workshop on China was based on this set of goals. A team of experts was assembled by the Poon Kam Kai Institute of Management at the University of Hong Kong and flown to GrandMet's headquarters in London. To ensure that the issues were raised from a front-line perspective, the majority were practitioners in key management positions.

Included was the executive director of one of Hong Kong's leading trading companies Wheelock; the general manager for business development at Courtaulds; the director of human resources at Ciba China; and the former business development manager at Coca Cola China. A video interview commissioned specially for the event with Shell's director for Central China provided the focus for discussions on marketing and branding.

Each session lasted an hour. But the speakers were instructed to speak only for 20 minutes and to pose at least three key issues on topics connected to joint venture negotiations, recruitment and training, distribution, intellectual property rights, market research, and Chinese business law.

The remainder of the hour was spent in facilitated discussion, with more effort than normal being devoted to capturing and recording the insights of senior managers from GrandMet's subsidiary firms. These included a number of front-line managers who were born in the region.

Two of the more important conclusions that emerged from this interchange were:

» *Corporate branding*: In the 1980s, GrandMet had been no more than a holding company, providing some centralized financial and other service support to its subsidiaries but leaving them free to establish their own brand identities. However, it rapidly emerged from the discussions that commercial umbrella organizations like Proctor & Gamble had fared better in negotiating favorable terms for the joint ventures their subsidiary companies wished to forge with Chinese partners by establishing a brand identity of their own with the provincial governments that were the main business brokers under the Communist system. Because China is run along centralized lines, the reputation of a single holding corporation can be used to endorse the products of a multitude of subsidiaries because, as one senior manager in the discussion group explained, Chinese government officials assume that executives in the holding group have the same level of control over the operation of the subsidiary as they have over manufacturing output in each of the factories in their province. A decision was made to explore the possibility of opening a series of representative offices on the mainland in GrandMet's own name.

» *Changing circumstances*: Both the commentators and the experienced line managers in the group stressed that circumstances in mainland China were changing rapidly. New "special regions" were being set up away from the coastline to encourage external investment in Central and Northern China and the state was actively investing in and supporting a new range of locally-run enterprises that would provide new opportunities for client-supplier relationships. (A good example being the Founder Group, founded by Beijing University, which was providing advanced Chinese language computer software in collaboration with Hewlett Packard – see Chapter 5.) Regular cross-subsidiary updates would be needed to keep the corporation as a whole in touch with these changes. It was decided that a think tank should be set up specifically to consider the implications of the latest developments in China, made up from participants on the Spearhead China program.

Both initiatives were well underway when successful merger negotiations with the Guinness corporation led to the establishment of the Diagio Group. The new conglomerate inherited the good work and many of the conclusions reached by the Spearhead China discussions have now resulted in Diagio initiatives.

NORTEL NETWORKS: FOSTERING INNOVATION IN THE FRONT LINE

Nortel Networks has been at the forefront of product development in the telecomms industry. During the 1990s, the company launched a number of schemes to provoke greater creativity among its staff.

A good example is the Business Ventures Group, an internal venturing scheme that allows employees with ideas for new startups to explore the practicalities in a secure environment with the right financial support and access to expertise, in return for a share in the equity, should the venture succeed. In 1996, for example, they helped two employees, Gord Larose and David Allan, to launch Channelware, a company renting software over the Internet, with bases in Ottawa, New York, San Francisco, and Los Angeles. It now employs over 60 staff.

Nortel helped out with office equipment, office space leases, and legal advice. Its technical experts worked with Larose and Allan to develop the software that enabled Channelware to deliver its services to customers. And it brokered the new venture into some of its largest customers. In return, it asked for a majority shareholding until 2000, when the venture was spun off. Nortel now owns 44% of the company,

Channelware's founders and staff about 20%, with the remainder shared among various other investors.

The scheme therefore allows Nortel's budding entrepreneurs the space and licence to experiment in a way that they would never get if they looked for conventional financial backing. "We let people refine their plans and pitch them to us again," says a member of the Business Venture Group's advisory board. "You don't get a second chance with venture capitalists."

Another initiative is the Intellectual Property Awards and Recognition Plan, launched in 1996. Benchmark studies in the late 1990s suggested to Nortel that it was successfully registering fewer patents than its principal competitors. The company sees the expansion and protection of its intellectual property rights as a key competitive tool. It was therefore keen to explore ways in which the challenge of developing, filing, and successfully registering patents for key products and technologies could be extended to a broader range of its research and scientific staff.

The aim of the Plan is two-fold:

» To encourage all research and scientific staff to become actively involved in developing, filing, and successfully registering patents for key products and technologies developed at its laboratories.
» By publicising successful patent applications, to emphasise the importance of intellectual property as a key competitive tool among all staff working for the company.

The Plan provides both monetary awards and public recognition for all staff involved in successful patent applications. There are four grades:

» *Patent Filing*. This rewards all staff involved in the development of a patent at the point at which it is filed. The award is made at the site at which the work is undertaken.
» *Patent Registering*. This rewards staff who have had a patent successfully registered.
» *Cumulative Awards*. This rewards staff who have been involved in a number of successful patent applications, usually between five and ten.
» *Significant patent awards*. This rewards staff who have been involved in the successful registering of a patent deemed to be

of particular value to the company. Examples include patents that have brought in substantial licensing revenues, formed the basis of an important industry standards, protected one of the company's core technologies or products, or received industry-wide recognition.

Staff receive a monetary award and a plaque highlighting their achievement. Presentations for the higher awards are made by a senior manager from the unit's national headquarters in the presence of other patent awardees and take place at sites of scientific or engineering significance. In the UK, which has spent £160 million alone on R&D, recent awards have taken place at Greenwich Laboratory, the Thames Barrier, and Bletchley Park, where the German Enigma code was cracked during the Second World War.

The awards are highlighted in the company's worldwide electronic newsletters and often form the basis for local or international press campaigns.

In the five years since the Plan was launched, there has been a significant increase in the number of patents registered across the company, not only in quantity but in quality. More time is now being given to assess and pass on the good practice associated with successful patent applications.

As Richard Epworth stresses, the initiative has not so much given new incentive to those of Nortel Networks' research/scientific staff that were already actively and regularly engaged in patent applications, but has broadened this to include the wider Nortel community.

"As front-line consultant, I got off on doing the work and I think the same is true of my colleagues. The money and the recognition were incidental to the satisfaction we got in breaking new ground. However the Plan has stimulated and intellectually engaged staff at the laboratories who were not previously engaged in this kind of work and given a much needed boost in recognition of the importance of our work to Nortel's staff generally.

Ewan Bewley also points out that there has been an important shift in thinking among Nortel Networks' line managers:

"There was a feeling that the time involved in developing and filing a patent was time the company couldn't afford. The Plan has illustrated that protecting and nurturing our intellectual property is not an incidental activity. It is the life and soul of our future. Winning this recognition alone has made the scheme worthwhile."

KEY LEARNING POINTS

» The role of the team leader or project manager is pivotal in ensuring a creative output from any initiative. He or she selects the members of the team, ensuring that there is the right diversity in deep knowledge and cultural or intellectual thinking, and shapes the way the group will work. The best groups adopt an inclusive style of working which does not let the pressure they work under prevent all members "having their say." (British Airways)

» Lateral thinking in research and experimentation in manufacturing industries is often inhibited by the cost of producing prototype components that may have to be ditched if the project is abandoned. Finding ways to reduce the "risk factor" of early experimentation, by reducing the cost of manufacturing these components, leads to bolder thinking. Siting experiments close to assembly lines where the practicality of early experiments can be tested produces a similar daring. (BMW)

» Left to their own devices, different divisions or subsidiaries will not share essential information. Workshops and think tanks that bring together managers from different parts of the organization to focus on specific challenges or goals that affect the organization as a whole is an essential part of any innovative strategy. (Grand Metropolitan/Diageo)

» "Intrapreneurialism" can be encouraged by corporate venturing schemes that enable staff to set up ventures of their own with corporate support and also recognition and reward schemes that help staff recognize the importance of extending and preserving the intellectual property of the organization. (Nortel Networks)

Key Concepts and Thinkers

» Creativity and leadership
» Teamwork and creativity
» Serendipity, cross-functional networking, and creativity
» How ideas are inspired (and constrained)
» How ideas are fostered and shaped

CREATIVITY AND LEADERSHIP

Most of the work on creativity and leadership has looked at the topic from two angles.

The first is how a leader is personally creative, in terms of how he or she takes decisions and thinks up ideas. During the early days of work on change management, inspired by the initiative of CEOs like General Electric's Jack Welch, The Body Shop's Anita Roddick, and Virgin's Richard Branson, the leader was held up as the visionary who determined the values and missions that would carry the organization forward.

Charles Handy, Europe's foremost guru, while still a professor at London Business School in 1987, defined the leader as the person who "shapes and shares a vision which gives point to the work of others." Part of his thesis was that the leader must live the vision:

> "He or she must not only believe in it but must be seen to believe in it. It is tempting credulity to proclaim a crusade for the impoverished from a luxury apartment. Effective leaders, we are told, exude energy. Energy comes easily if you love your cause. Effective leaders have integrity. Integrity, being true to yourself, comes naturally if you live for your vision. In other words, the vision cannot be something thought up in the drawing office. To be real, it has to come from the deepest parts of you, from an inner system of belief. The total pragmatist cannot be a transforming leader."

Part of this deeply personal role is to be the fount of all ideas. **Jack Welch**, rather than his production experts, thought up and pioneered the concept of the boundaryless organization. **Anita Roddick**, not her R&D managers, traveled around the primitive tribes of the developing world looking for ideas for new products. **Michael Eisner**, the man who turned around the Disney Corporation in the 1980s, nailed his colors to the wall very clearly in an interview for *Fortune* in 1989. "To me the pursuit of ideas is the only thing that matters. You can always find capable people to do almost everything else."

The second approach has been to look at how leaders encourage creativity in others. Teamworking expert **Meredith Belbin** (see below) has long nursed concerns about the disempowering influence of "solo" leaders, principally because they collect acolytes who will not challenge their ideas rather than talent that would build on them. "The more macho the leader the more submissive the followers tend to be . . . the effect can be so powerful that the very culture of the company may shift to reflect the solo leader's favored style of managing."

This is borne out by **Marsha Sinetar's** work on creative entrepreneurs at the Massachusetts Institute of Technology (see Chapter 3 and below). She found that creatives who either found their own company or are appointed into a CEO role often display personal characteristics that actively discourage creativity among their subordinates. These include condescending and dictatorial behavior and an unwillingness or inability to delegate.

In place of these self-obsessed soloists should be what Meredith Belbin calls 'team leaders': people whose primary role is to unleash the creative potential of the organization, helping front line workers develop their own solutions to the challenges facing the organization rather than imposing the solutions from the top.

Tudor Rickards at the University of Manchester raised the issue in 1988 in his best-selling book *Creativity and Problem-Solving at Work*:

"The obvious way to be creative [as a leader] is through example – sparking off ideas which can be developed and implemented. Unfortunately, this strategy rarely succeeds. If the 'creative' leader is truly outstanding as a creative individual, he or she is rarely equally able to manage the creative ideas, and might be better off as a team member producing an outstanding flow of stimuli. If, on the other hand, the leader is no better at producing ideas than the others, then the unconscious favoring given to the leader's ideas demotivates the others."

Rickards proposed a quite different way of operating as a creative leader. This is to concentrate on "ideas about ideas." To develop this kind of leadership style

"you must learn to pay attention to the signals which people give out regarding their needs and beliefs. You must learn that sometimes the best way to help people is not to supply our own solutions – even if it is quite obvious to you what needs to be done. Creative leaders make things happen, but their approach is more subtle – more like a midwife than a surgeon.''

This role has been fleshed out in more recent years by **Ronald Heifetz**, Director of the Leadership Education Project at Harvard University's John F. Kennedy School of Government. Instead of defining the problems facing the organization and then providing the solutions, Heifetz argues that modern leaders should use their "helicopter" perspective to identify the challenges and frame the key questions and issues that the rest of the workforce should grapple with.

The effective leader frees up their front-line workers from the constraints of unnecessary rules and regulations, challenging current roles but resisting pressure to define new roles quickly. At the same time, he or she keeps the organization in a constant state of flux by throwing out a stream of new goals or challenges, exposing conflict or letting it emerge rather than continually attempting to restore order.

Heifetz compares the process to that of regulating a pressure cooker by turning up the heat while simultaneously allowing some of the steam to escape. If the pressure exceeds the cooker's capacity, Heifetz stresses, the cooker can blow up. However, nothing cooks without some heat.

TEAMWORK AND CREATIVITY

Teamwork, like leadership, is a consistently popular and fast-moving topic of management debate and its links with creativity have been the focus for a great deal of good academic work in recent years.

The father of team role theory is Dr **Meredith Belbin**, originally based at Cambridge University and since 1988 the founder of Belbin Associates with his son Nigel. In his widely-read book *Management Teams: Why they Succeed or Fail* and its successor *Team Roles at Work* Belbin identified nine roles that need to be played if teams are to successfully fulfil their goals. These are explored in greater detail in another ExpressExec title, *Teamworking*, but, from the perspective we are exploring, three roles are identified by Belbin as being particularly creative.

» The first are "plants," described as creative, imaginative, and unortho-dox. They come up with the solutions to difficult problems but often lack good communication or management skills.

» Also high in creative skills are "resource investigators," described as extrovert, enthusiastic, and communicative. They explore opportu-nities thrown up by the team and develop the right contacts, but often lose interest once their initial enthusiasm has passed.

» Finally there are "shapers," described as dynamic, outgoing, and highly-strung; often prone to provocation and short-lived bursts of temper. They challenge views and find ways around obstacles.

Belbin is at pains to stress that, while some people might be better suited to specific roles than others, this does not mean they are in a psychological straitjacket. The labels "plant" or "shaper" refer to roles, not people. Individuals can choose to play one role or another according to the team's needs.

This is entirely different from the new stream of work on "hot-groups," where all members of the team are presumed to be "creative." The assumption here is that, by virtue of their heightened insight and lateral mindedness, the group operates in a different way to workaday teams. Here is a typical description of how a creative group works, by Anthony Jay, BBC producer and the writer of the UK hit television series *Yes Minister*:

> "Creative groups use up a lot of energy. Often they work hard and long and late, and they cannot be supervised, checked on for punctuality and efficiency, as the more routine performers can. It is often impossible anyway, but when morale is high it is also unnecessary because the work becomes a great source of satisfaction. For this reason, they respond better to encouragement and enthusiasm than many others. But most of all they respond to success, to the visible, objective success of what they are doing."

But the danger with "hot-groups" is that they tend to become over-baked. Telling some teams or groups they are more creative than others fosters the same elitist culture in an organization as telling it to individuals (see Chapter 3). Over time the perspective of its members will homogenize, reducing its creative output, and the team will become increasingly protective of its work, cutting down its willingness to share.

In the UK, Meredith Belbin is currently pioneering the concept of the "progression helix" which will enable teams to make better informed decisions based on shared information without the delays and obstructions of upward referral.

Based on a study of termite nests during a visit to Northern Australia in 1993, this postulates that the creative potential of any organization should be based around a standing strategic team or "co-operating caste" that are recruited, trained, and nurtured in much the same way as high-flyers currently are. However, to prevent the team becoming ossified in its decision-making (or, in anthropological terms, biologically unadaptable) the caste should be constantly freshened by new recruits with specialist knowledge or new thinking that is specifically relevant to the current challenges faced by the organization.

Membership of the caste is not based on rank. Recruits can enter at different points and in particular positions, moving forward towards seniority, as they prove their value by their contributions to the teams. Membership of teams can overlap and interact as in a hive or anthill, with the difference that with the human capacity for managing strategy and change, they can also work currently.

Teams operating in this fashion, Belbin claims, can furnish a wider range of ideas and innovations than a static group, can shorten decision-making times, and can expose concerns that might be hidden by traditional management anxious to maintain a favorable image:

"Visually the movements [of the members of these teams] are as difficult to track as those moving within a honey bee's nest or a termite's mound: there is no allotted territory within which the individual is confined. In a developing and fast-moving human organization, memberships of teams can overlap. At the same time, different strategic teams can also act concurrently and are empowered to make decisions that fall within their orbit. There is no longer a need to wait until certain senior figures make themselves available."

Dorothy Leonard, a professor at Harvard Business School, argues that the label "creative" is misleading and elitist. Any team can be creative in the way it works provided it obeys a few basic rules.

The most important, according to the work she has undertaken monitoring teams of all kinds, is that members are selected for their diversity of "deep" knowledge and different cultural and intellectual ways of thinking.

Managers who dislike conflict – or value only their own approach – actively avoid selecting diverse team members because it will lead to a clash of ideas. They select and reward people of a particular type, usually people like themselves. The team, and ultimately the organization as a whole, then becomes a victim of what Leonard calls "comfortable clone syndrome." Team members share similar interests and training, and everyone thinks alike. Because ideas all pass through similar cognitive screens, only familiar ones survive. The result is a total lack of creative output.

SERENDIPITY, CROSS-FUNCTIONAL NETWORKING, AND CREATIVITY

Casual, unfocused interchanges between individuals with the right combination of knowledge and perspectives has long been recognized as a primary source of new ideas. A survey of research engineers in the late 1980s by the Massachusetts Institute of Technology found that 80% of ideas that led to breakthrough products were sparked off over a chat next to the coffee machine or some other corporate social facility.

The MIT study also pinpointed the workspace features that are most likely to cut dead any instinct an individual might have to get up and wander over to a colleague's desk to check out an idea or point of detail. These include long corridors, lifts, closed doors, walks between buildings, and the need to dress up.

Not surprisingly, the issue of creative interchange and workspace design has been a focal point for architectural studies. Dr **Tadeusz Grajeweski** and Professor **Bill Hillier** of the Bartlett School of Architecture and Planning at the University of London became interested in the topic in a study published in the early 1990s: "The Social Potential of Buildings."

Like the MIT study, this suggested that a far greater link existed between an individual's output and his or her movement around the building than had previously been recognized or allowed for by workspace design. But the sudden impulse that generated this movement is liable to interruption by any number of environmental factors.

A good example is fluctuating temperature in a temperate climate. An extract from the report reads:

> "Unfortunately, the English climate dictates that outdoor meeting spaces can only be used for a comparatively short part of the year . . . on warm days you are much more likely to stop and chat than on a cold day. An outdoor space is (also) likely to have a strong detrimental effect on movement between different houses. Having to put on a coat and negotiate several drafty lobbies will in itself deter people from undertaking journeys . . . [As a result] there will be a strong drop in communication between the different houses."

Both studies inspired an innovative use of workspace design by large corporations. The MIT study was drawn on heavily in the design of a new R&D center by BMW, close to its corporate headquarters in Munich. The Bartlett research inspired the design of British Airways' Waterside Centre at Heathrow. These initiatives are covered in detail in the ExpressExec title *The Innovative Individual* in Chapter 4 and Chapter 7).

However more recent research has indicated strongly that imaginative workspace design is not enough in itself to get people to share and exchange. The University of Strathclyde in Glasgow conducted an experiment in conjunction with the Scottish Enterprise Agency in 1997. Some 70 of the Agency's staff, working in four teams, worked in new offices designed in the manner recommended by the MIT and Bartlett studies, with communal social facilities and areas specifically designed for private study, teamworking, and "hive" working.

The study found that while communication between members of the same teams improved markedly through using the new facilities, communication between members of different teams remained as furtive as ever, with little information or knowledge being exchanged.

What is additionally required, according to **Morten Hansen** of Harvard Business School and **Bolko von Oetinger** of the Boston Consulting Group are "T-shaped" managers. These are executives who are prepared to share knowledge and ideas across the whole organization (the horizontal part of the "T") while remaining fiercely committed to the performance of their team or business unit (the vertical part).

Studies of teams and hot-groups in companies such as Siemens, BP Exploration, and steelmakers Ispat International show that considerable tensions are brought about by the need to reconcile the split loyalties this requires. A typical T-shaped manager, for example, must collaborate in a peer group, connect people from different parts of the company and give or take advice from other teams or business units.

For this exchange to become routine and commonplace, organizations need to identify and promote those managers who are best placed to bridge the divide. **Karen Stephenson**, a professor at the University of California, Los Angeles, found in research with the IBM Advanced Business Unit, that informal networks control the daily life of organizations.

The principal figures in these networks – the people who shape the conversation in the corridors, play the role in succession planning, and decide who stays and who goes during mergers or downsizing exercises – are those best able to play what Hansen and von Oetinger call T-shaped roles.

Particularly important are the gate-keepers – managers who through a small number of relationships link the various parts of the business – and the pulse-takers – managers whose cross-functional responsibilities cut across all hierarchies and whose web of relationships allows them to know what everyone in the organization is thinking or feeling.

Gaining the support of such people, Stephenson argues, is crucial if a change or initiative is to succeed. A forward-thinking chief executive, for example, might want to test the ground before introducing an innovative new way of working. The gate-keepers would be used to spread the news about the impending change on a semi-formal basis, and later the pulse-takers would report the "word on the ground."

HOW IDEAS ARE INSPIRED (AND CONSTRAINED)

Much of the work that has been undertaken on how ideas are inspired (explored in more detail in the ExpressExec title *The Innovative Individual*) originated from work published by a series of psychologists in the 1950s and 1960s.

The first, **Francis E Vaughan**, stressed that we are only conscious of a fraction of what we know and that our minds are constantly processing information without us being conscious of the fact. The second, **Alex Osborn**, in his seminal book *Creative Imagination*, stressed that, as a consequence, we are all sitting on a "volcano" of ideas and insights that we are often prevented from realizing or sharing either because we lack the right level of self-confidence or because we think those around us – particularly work colleagues – will dismiss out of hand.

Osborn also argued that "wild" ideas are often the most valuable because, even if they are impractical, they place ourselves and those around us "outside our box" and therefore act a bridge to ideas that *are* practical but are born from a different perspective of the reality in hand. The key to a creative exchange, he stressed, is not the *quality* of ideas generated by any discussion but the *volume*.

Our own work on this subject, conducted for the Roffey Park Institute in the UK, confirmed much of what Vaughan and Osborn concluded. In a survey of 120 senior managers and directors, many with a track record of innovation and creative thinking, we found that over 90% thought up their best business idea away from the workplace. Many deliberately focused their creative thinking in a specific time or space (driving into work, before they went to sleep, having a shower, taking the dog for a walk, etc.). They nurtured this "resource" as a means of "fast-tracking" their creative juices because it was somewhere or sometime where they could "drift and dream" (driving, showering, and walking being activities, for example, which are often undertaken on autopilot).

We also found that the same group drew their inspiration from a wide variety of sources, many being non-work-related. These included insights drawn from personal or professional networking, attending a conference or workshop, private reading, personal leisure pursuits, community activities, or family life. The most creative ideas often occurred from insights or perspectives on work drawn from, for example, reading a biography, playing sport, or bringing up children.

Most of this work is focused on the cognitive and intellectual processes of the mind. However a new stream of research in the past few years has focused on the inter-relationship between intellect, emotion, and spirituality in business decision-making.

US psychologist **Daniel Goleman** looked at the profiles of top performers in 500 companies worldwide and found that a high IQ got the best managers only to the first rung of their chosen careers. After that, personal qualities such as an ability to empathize with others and grasp the bigger picture counted for much more than analytical skills.

A long-term research project at Harvard University has been examining the neuro-biological basis on the workings of the brain and how this influences day-to-day decision-making. The two professors representing the business school, **Michael Jensen** and **Chris Argyris**, are using the results to determine why chief executives persist in making decisions that are bound to damage their companies. They have already concluded that the unconscious mechanisms that generate a "fight or flight" response also generate emotionally defensive behavior in humans.

Ironically, it is the same chain reaction – where the amygdala that registers emotion in the brain kicks in before the cortex which is the source of rational thought – that psychologists like **Francis Vaughan** point out create the instinct or "gut feel" that is now recognized as an integral part of effective decisions.

Danah Zohar, a physicist and philosopher turned management guru, has taken this line of research to its most recent stage. She argues that the neurons that determine our behavior are capable of oscillating in unison, which accounts for our ability to be insightful, creative, and ready to challenge existing ideas and orthodoxies.

People with what she terms "highly-developed spiritual intelligence" are more open to diversity, have a greater tendency to ask "why," and have the capacity to face and use adversity. They actively seek uncomfortable situations because they recognize that their ability to interpret the environment around them will be enhanced as a result.

HOW IDEAS ARE FOSTERED AND SHAPED

Our own research on this subject, once again conducted for the UK's Roffey Park Institute, is summarized in Chapter 2. In short, a detailed surveillance of creative projects in a variety of disparate organizations threw up a number of key roles in how the ideas that were the source of the initiative were shaped, sponsored, supported, and informed.

Very few of the tasks we identified are currently undertaken by managers as a "mandated" part of their role. The result is that the license to experiment and play with ideas, which is an essential foundation for creativity, is lacking in their staff.

The consequences were highlighted vividly in a recent experiment conducted by **Amy Edmondson** and **Stefan Thomke**, both assistant professors at Harvard Business School. Edmondson and Thomke monitored the introduction of a new Website at a large US Midwestern healthcare organization. The Website was designed to provide administrators and caregivers with a single access point for retrieving the most up-to-date clinical information.

Previously, healthcare workers had to log on to several different systems to access patient information that may or may not have been updated with data from other departments. Because there was no formal training course for the system, employees had to experiment with it to gain proficiency.

The two researchers found that individuals were more willing to experiment with the new system – to try out different software applications and to test system features – when their departmental managers did two things: explicitly state that making mistakes would be okay, and refraining from punishing employees for errors.

Managers who gave mixed signals, such as verbally encouraging experimentation while maintaining a reward system that punished failure, created confusion and mistrust among their staff. Experimentation was much rarer in these departments and the effects of an inconsistent message were particularly strong among junior employees who felt they had more to lose by getting the message wrong.

KEY LEARNING POINTS

» Creative leadership in modern corporations is more about helping others to make creative decisions than making them yourself. Framing the challenges and goals facing the organization, assessing effectively the level of pressure the organization can bear, and freeing up the organization from rules and processes that inhibit creativity are the hallmarks of the best contemporary leaders.

» Creative groups are driven by their output and intellectual engagement. Left untouched over time they tend to ossify. The key is to select members with highly diversified "deep" knowledge and cultural or intellectual ways of thinking, and to keep membership and the agenda fresh. Project managers and team leaders have a key role to play in achieving this.

» Networking and sharing across difference functions is a key characteristic of creative organizations. Those managers that bridge different parts of the organization - the "gate-keepers" and "pulse-takers" - play an important role in helping the organization develop and stay fresh.

» The mind constantly processes information that we are not conscious of. As a consequence, inspiration for creative business ideas often occurs outside the workplace and is informed by activities and interests that are often not related to work. Intellectual capability needs to be tempered by emotional and spiritual maturity if an individual is to achieve his or her full creative potential.

» Many of the most important tasks related to shaping and fostering ideas are not a "mandated" part of a manager's role. The experimentation and play that is so important to creativity will not occur unless managers match what they say with what they and the organization do to reward and recognize risk taking, whether or not it is successful.

Resources

» Books
» Journals
» Research

This chapter lists books, articles, and Websites which you may find helpful in furthering your study of creativity. Some related publications are listed in Chapter Nine of the ExpressExec title *The Innovative Individual*.

BOOKS

In addition to those previously mentioned within the chapters.

General reading

» Kennedy, C. (2001) *The Next Big Idea: Managing in the Digital Economy*, Random House, New York.

Kennedy is the leading authority on the work of the world's leading business gurus – she is also author of *Managing with the Gurus* (Century). This new book looks at the history of the "big" idea in business – covering Taylorism, total quality management, business process re-engineering, and emotional intelligence – and looks ahead to the broader social issues companies will have to confront as part of their greater global influence on people's lives. The chapter on how ideas are developed in organizations, which covers new concepts created by Toyota, General Electric, and Shell (among others), is particularly good.

» Leonard, D. & Swap, W. (1999) *When Sparks Fly: Igniting Creativity in Groups*, Harvard Business Press, Cambridge, MA.

Dorothy Leonard, a professor of business administration at Harvard Business School, is the leading authority on creative interchanges in teams (see Chapter 8). This is not an academic book, though, but a practical handbook containing a wealth of exercises and insights that team leaders, project managers, and participants in brainstorms can use to foster a freer flow of ideas. She covers issues like the value of incubation (sleeping on it), cool-hunting (seeking out street-wise ideas) and devil-advocating (encouraging creative dissent). The book also stresses the need for team leaders to go beyond simply seeking and tapping a few "creatives" in the group and to ignite creativity in everyone.

» Belbin, R.M. (1998) *The Coming Shape of the Organisation*, Butterworth Heinemann, Oxford.

Meredith Belbin has been the leading thinker on teamwork for over 30 years, and this latest book was inspired by a study of termite nests on a visit to northern Australia. Belbin thinks we have a lot to learn from the way insects organize their lives. The book is a bit long on analogy and short on practicalities, but stripping away the pseudo anthropology, he argues that insect societies work because they are run by a flexible "caste" or oligarchy, carefully developed by a sort of "high flying" process, which is prevented from ossifying by a constant influx of new members promoted on merit. This is not a book for those who want to cut to the quick, but it is stimulating if you like looking at organizational theory from a different perspective.

» Robbins, H. & Finlry, M. (1999) *Why Teams Don't Work: What Went Wrong and How to Make It Right*, Orion Business Paperbacks.

Harvey Robbins is a clinical psychologist who works with organizations in creating effective group work and this book is, well, a bit clinical. It lacks the creative imagery and colourful analogy of Dorothy Leonard's book on the same subject (see above) but it does cover all the bases. The chapter on communication shortfalls in particularly good. It is a comprehensive look at the subject aimed at people who want checklists, do's and don'ts, and blow-by-blow guidance.

» Kelly, T. with Littman, J. (2001) *The Art of Innovation: Lessons in Creativity from IDEO, America's Leading Design Firm*, Doubleday/Currency Books, New York.

IDEO is one of the world's leading design firms, responsible for developing, among other things, the Polaroid I-Zone Camera and Crest Toothpaste's Neat Squeeze tube. The founder David Kelly is the epitome of West Coast new thinking, and this book, written by his brother Tom, the firm's general manager, stresses that you shouldn't try to imitate the company's rules for success without changing your culture first. Being a design genius is great, he argues, but not at the expense of the team.

» Earle, N. & Keen, P. (2000) *From. com to. profit: Inventing Business Models That Deliver Value and Profit*, Jossey-Bass, San Francisco.

This book links strategy to the "big idea." The point of strategy is to help individuals choose between competing priorities. And according to the authors, the big idea or dream, the company's ambition for the future, can promote a climate of values that helps people make choices for themselves – whether or not to commit to the organization. How people see the future of the organization, individually and collectively, will determine whether it achieves its goals. In this sense, as in politics, the 'vision thing' is the key to strategy. Strategy today is nothing without the passion of the people implementing and building on it.

» O'Shea, J. & Madigan, C. (1999) *Dangerous Company: The Consulting Powerhouses and The Businesses They Save and Ruin*, Nicholas Brealey, London.

Though the role of consulting firms as ideas creators is limited to one or two chapters, notably one on the Boston Consulting Group (BCG), this book gives a fabulous inside view of how the big hitters do (or do not) work with their clients. The authors confirm one of our own conclusions – that consultancy – client relationships work best not when the consultancy is forcing to foist its own ideas on the client but when it helps the client place its own concepts and strategies in a broader context or perspective. The debunking of the BCG matrix – dogs, stars, and all – and business process re-engineering, which scored a 70% failure in the organizations in which it was introduced, does more than enough to convince that the big firms should concentrate on analysis and implementation at a micro level and leave big ideas to the academics and the practitioners.

» Langdon, K. (2001) *Smart Things to Know About Decision Making*, Capstone/Wiley, Oxford.

Langdon is the author of a host of books about practical ideas, including *The 100 Greatest Business Ideas of All Time* and *The 100 Greatest Ideas for Building Your Career*. This latest book covers a number of useful tips for the individual, from formal business trees to backing a hunch. One of the better 'how to's on the market.

Business from a non-business perspective

In the past decade, there has been an outpouring of books that look at the role of the manager, leader, or organization from the perspective of non-business disciplines – whether it be history, philosophy, the physical sciences, or art.

Here is a selection. They all provide the opportunity to look at common business challenges issues from a different perspective – but bear in mind the caveats we made in the chapters.

» Adair, J. (1989) *Great Leaders*, Talbot Adair Press. Guildford, UK.
» Roberts, W. (1994) *Victory Secrets of Attila the Hun*, Dell Publishing, Washington, DC.
» Morris, T. (1997) *If Aristotle Ran General Motors: The New Soul of Business*, Henry Holt & Co., New York.
» Whitney, J. & Packer, T. (2000) *Power Plays: Shakespeare's Lessons in Leadership and Management*, MacMillan, Basingstoke, UK.
» Krause, D.G. (1995) *Sun Tzu: The Art of War for Executives*, Berkley Publishing Group, New York.
» Machiavelli, N. *Power: Get It, Use It, Keep It*, Profile Books, London.

JOURNALS

Harvard Business Review

In recent years, this noteworthy journal has focused its attention on issues relating to creativity, innovation, and ideas development. The best articles include:

» Leonard, D. and Straus, S (1997) "Putting your company's whole brain to work," *Harvard Business Review*, July-August. (Introduction: *"Conflict is essential to innovation. The key is to make the abrasion creative."*)
» Amabile, T.M. (1998) "How to kill creativity," *Harvard Business Review*, September-October. (Introduction: *"Answer: Keep doing what you you're doing. Or, if you want to spark innovation, rethink how you motivate, reward, and assign work to people."*)
» Drucker, P.F. (1999) "Managing oneself," *Harvard Business Review*, March-April. (Introduction: *"Success in the knowledge economy comes to those who know themselves – their strengths, their values, and how they best perform."*)
» Hansen, M.T., Nohria, N. & Tierney, T. (1999) "What's your strategy for managing knowledge?" *Harvard Business Review*, March-April. (Introduction: "Some *companies automate knowledge management; others rely on their people to share knowledge through more*

traditional means. Emphasizing the wrong approach – or trying to pursue both at the same time – can quickly undermine your business.")

» Chan Kim, W. & Maubourgne, R. (2000) "Knowing a winning business idea when you see one," *Harvard Business Review*, September-October. (Introduction: *"Identifying which business ideas have real commercial potential is one of the most difficult challenges that executives face. Three tools – to determine utility, price, and business model – can help them invest wisely.*")

» Eppinger, S.D. (2001) "Innovation at the speed of information," *Harvard Business Review*, January. (Introduction: *"Developing a new product involves trial and error, but beyond a certain point, redesign becomes wasteful. A practical and proven tool, the* Design Structure Matrix, *can help streamline the way a company works.*")

» Thomke, S. (2001) "Enlightened experimentation: The new imperative for innovation," *Harvard Business Review*, February. (Introduction: *"The high cost of experimentation has long put a damper on companies' attempts to create great new products. But new technologies are making it easier than ever to conduct complex experiments quickly and cheaply.*")

» Hayashi, A.M. (2001) "When to trust your gut," *Harvard Business Review*, February. (Introduction: *"How do business executives make crucial decisions? Often by relying on their keen intuitive skills, otherwise known as their 'gut'. But what exactly is gut instinct and how does it work? Scientists have recently uncovered some provocative clues that may change the way you work.*")

» Urch Druskat, V. & Wolff, S.B. (2001) "Building the emotional intelligence of groups," *Harvard Business Review*, March. (Introduction: *"By now, most executives have accepted that emotional intelligence is as critical as IQ to an individual's effectiveness. But much of the important work in organisations is done in teams. New research uncovers what emotional intelligence at a group level looks like – and how to achieve it.*")

» Charan, R. (2001) "Conquering a culture of indecision," *Harvard Business Review*, April. (Introduction: *"Some people just can't make up their minds. The same goes for companies – and their performance suffers as a result. But new research shows that*

*leaders can eradicate indecision by transforming the tone and
content of everyday conversations at their organizations.''*)

MORE ABOUT THE AUTHORS' RESEARCH

The research highlighted in Chapters 2, 6, and 8 was conducted as
part of a long-term programme at the UK Roffey Park Institute in
Horsham on tracking innovation in the organization. The full findings
are highlighted in two reports:

» *Innovation at the Top: Where Directors Get their Ideas From*

and

» *Entering Tiger Country: How Ideas Are Shaped in Organisations*

Both are available from the Publications Department, Roffey Park Institute, Forest Road, Horsham, West Sussex RH12 4TD United Kingdom
Tel: 44(0)1293 851644 Fax: 44(0) 1293 851565. www.roffeypark.com;
email: info@roffeypark.com

Ten Ways to Foster Creativity

1 Treat creativity as a collective force
2 Treat creativity as a collective process
3 Free up the organization's processes
4 Free up the organization's thinking
5 Match words with deeds
6 Draw on external "sounding boards"
7 See customers and staff as two sides of the same technological coin
8 Make internal investment less of a "zero sum game"
9 Do not lose your corporate memory
10 Provide the frame rather than painting the picture

1. TREAT CREATIVITY AS A COLLECTIVE FORCE

Targeting a small creative elite is shortsighted – they may leave to pursue their own ends, regardless of how much money and status you throw at them – and winds up disempowering everyone else. There is no conclusive evidence that some people are more creative than others, only that some people respond more creatively to certain working environments than others. Change the environment and you improve people's capacity to respond.

2. TREAT CREATIVITY AS A COLLECTIVE PROCESS

Breakthroughs in products, services, and ways of working may start with the insight or idea of an individual. But the process of making that idea "real" involves teamwork and project management. Contributions will be made from a variety of internal or external professionals, either involved directly in shaping the original concept or acting as sponsors, champions, or sounding boards. At the moment, the task of fostering, championing, supporting, and shaping the ideas of colleagues and subordinates is not seen as an essential team or management role. It needs to be.

3. FREE UP THE ORGANISATION'S PROCESSES

Research by Marsha Sinetar at the Massachusetts Institute of Technology suggest that some people need freedom to be creative in how they undertake their work, in focusing on issues they find particularly interesting, and in asking awkward questions or challenging norms. Others, as in the case of administrators and professional support staff at British Airways' Waterside headquarters (see Chapter 2 and Chapter 7), find these freedoms a threat. Work practices need to be sufficiently flexible to provide free thinkers with the discretion they require to follow up hunches and challenge orthodoxies while providing other staff with the continuity they need to follow through and support the results.

4. FREE UP THE ORGANIZATION'S THINKING

Freed-up processes require freed-up thinking. The volume of ideas is often more important than their individual qualities. Wild ideas and reverse logic may not be practical but they get people to think outside their box. Coming to the "right" solution too quickly may be counterproductive. Looking at a problem from a different perspective – whether the difference be of industry, culture, or personal interest – may cut through vested or rigid thinking. In this sense, recruiting for diversity (see Chapter 5) is a creative rather than simply an ethical measure.

5. MATCH WORDS WITH DEEDS

Walking the talk is essential. Studies by Harvard Business School (see Chapter 8) suggest that managers who give mixed signals, such as verbally encouraging experimentation while maintaining a reward system that punishes failure, create confusion and mistrust among staff. Risk-taking and trials are rarer in their departments and the constraints are particularly noticeable among junior staff, who have more to lose by public failure.

By contrast, schemes like the Intellectual Property Awards and Recognition Plan at Nortel Networks (see Chapter 7) actively encourage staff to push out the boundaries of the company's knowledge and see the expansion of its intellectual property rights as a crucial competitive tool. The money people receive under the plan is incidental in significance compared with the incentive it provides to calculated risk-taking and the message it sends out that creativity matters.

6. DRAW ON EXTERNAL "SOUNDING BOARDS"

Our own research suggests that organizations often use external advisors or experts such as consultants, academics, and non-executive directors in the wrong way. We live in the world of the "next big idea," with academics and consultants vying with each other to come up with "branded" solutions to the challenges facing industry. In the past ten years, for example, business consultancies and schools have worked their way through (among others) leanness, empowerment, time-based competition, business process re-engineering, emotional intelligence, empowerment, and complex adaptive systems.

Organizations are more than capable of finding their own solutions, but the narrow perspective they operate from means these ideas need to be assessed and re-evaluated from a broader viewpoint. Academics, consultants, and non-executive directors, if well chosen, can provide this perspective, pointing front-line managers to similar initiatives in other organizations and benchmarking the concepts against current industry or sector good practice.

7. SEE CUSTOMERS AND STAFF AS TWO SIDES OF THE SAME TECHNOLOGICAL COIN

In the "new" economy, innovation is frequently technology-driven (see Chapter 4). But the rapid take-up of e-mail and the Internet in the office and at home has left a generational divide in terms of how comfortable different people are with the technology.

The capacity for using Websites and intranets to conduct interactive dialog at a distance, for example, is constrained only by people's willingness to see this as a substitute for human contact. This applies as much to whether they are communicating with colleagues at another worksite as it does if they are buying a complex product or service on a personal computer for the home. Unless the organization is targeting a customer base which is highly proficient in technology, its own workforce will provide a good benchmark of the comfort factor that will apply in new products or services that are delivered or developed over the Net.

8. MAKE INTERNAL INVESTMENT LESS OF A "ZERO SUM GAME"

Ideas-driven companies, with or without formal R&D, will have to choose at some point which gestating projects to back and which to abandon. In doing so, they will certainly apply formal measures to assess the viability of each idea in terms of performance, simplicity, convenience risk, image, or environmental friendliness (see Chapter 6).

However, these decisions do not have to be a zero sum game. Organizations like GlaxoSmithKline (see Chapter 6) and BMW (see Chapter 7) have found that abandoned projects often yield insights and the germs of ideas that, used in a different context, lead to breakthroughs. Encouraging experimentation by reducing the cost of failure (in financial and career terms) and ensuring that people are recognized and rewarded for transferring knowledge pays dividends to the long-term creativity of the firm.

9. DO NOT LOSE YOUR CORPORATE MEMORY

People who have made a creative contribution to your organization move on: because they want to further their careers, because of downsizing, to start a family. Lose them and you are in danger of losing your corporate memory. Therefore encourage all staff on creative projects to use the latest technology to capture what happens. Focus not just on the output but the thinking that went into it and encourage staff to use a narrative style that, as in the case of 3M (see Chapter 6) sets the stage, defines the tensions, and describes the resolution.

If former employees on creative projects are willing and able, buy them back from time to time to brief their successors and ensure that their successors keep in touch with the latest developments in the field. Make more of an effort to do this in a recession. Economic downturns are the time when large corporations most lose touch with technological advances and changes in the marketplace.

10. PROVIDE THE FRAME RATHER THAN PAINTING THE PICTURE

Traditionally business and project leaders defined the problem and came up with the solution. Now they define the problem and let others come up with the solution – and they perform this task with a much lighter touch.

Rather than using the definition as a straitjacket, it should be no more than a starting point: a personal view, informed by the "helicopter" vision the leader has of the project or the firm, of what challenges, issues, and questions are involved.

Creativity is about change. The best business leaders, operating at any level, are consummate change managers. They let the project or the organization feel external pressures within a range it can stand, challenge current roles and resist pressure to define new roles quickly, and challenge unproductive rules and processes. As Warren Bennis of the University of Southern California concludes: "A leader challenges the *status quo*; a manager accepts it."

Frequently Asked Questions (FAQs)

Q1: What is the difference between creativity and innovation?

A: There is no clear-cut answer to this because there is no consensus of expert opinion. The two terms, whether used as nouns or adjectives, are interchangeable in most conference presentations and books or articles.

However, when experts and practitioners are taxed on the subject, creativity tends to be used to describe a dynamic that takes place between individuals or groups, while innovation is used to describe the collective capability of an organization to use this dynamic effectively. In other words, creativity describes the potential, innovation describes the result.

By way of illustration, here is a recent description of each term by a front-line manager:

"Business creativity is about how you work with other people, how people work in groups, how people manage change, how people assume control over their working lives, and how well they are able to integrate their working lives into their whole life."

Ruth McCall, founder, Cambridge Animation Systems

"Innovation is the constant search for a fresh or novel approach to every aspect of running the business, whether that is in new or existing products; new techniques or new raw materials; new strategies or new ways of working. It is both a science and an art and knowing how and when to apply these is often the difference between success and failure."

Keith Oates, former deputy chairman, Marks & Spencer

Q2: How does inspiration occur?

A: "I can see the light going on in my head but do not know where the current comes from" says one of the hundreds of senior managers we have interviewed on this subject.

There appear to be three factors in play when inspiration "strikes."

» First, there is a nagging or pressing business problem that needs to be solved. It is very difficult to be creative in a vacuum.
» Second, the individual is in an environment where he or she can "drift and dream." This varies from one person to another but common examples include driving to and from work, taking a shower, in the process of going to sleep or when waking up, or while taking the dog for a walk. The key thing in all these activities is that they are undertaken on autopilot, allowing the individual to dance around the subject without making it the main focus.
» Third, inspiration is drawn, while in this drifting state, from insights or perspectives that often have nothing to do with work. Break-throughs often occur when people look at a common business problem from the perspective of a different "world." Common examples include insights derived from professional or personal networking, attending conferences or workshops, private reading, personal leisure activities, community activities, and family life.

The important overriding fact to take on board is that the mind is constantly processing information when we are not conscious of it doing so, even when we are sleeping. Inspiration occurs when an event or train of thought allows us to tap into this thought bank. But, as the French novelist Marcel Proust stresses in *Remembrance of Things Past*, this is not something we can consciously will to occur. An unrelated thought or action is what usually acts as the trigger.

Q3: Who owns an idea?

A: This is becoming more of a tricky question to answer as intellectual property has assumed a greater commercial importance. As we describe in Chapter 2, almost all creative breakthroughs in organizations start with an insight or idea thought up by an individual or small set of individuals. But this acts as no more than a "spark" for a much more complex process of shaping, testing, and refining which can involve anything from a small project development team to hundreds of people.

The law as it stands protects individuals by allowing them to establish copyright or a patent over a defined product or body of work. But you cannot protect an idea and once it is shared in the organization, it is in effect common property. That is why people are so wary about contributing creatively to organizations and why organizations need to pay more attention to tackling the reluctance.

Q4: Can you pay people to be creative?

A: The last question inevitably leads to this one. Hard practice and plentiful research shows that there are a small number of "creatives" that are motivated simply by the challenge and the task in hand. As Marsha Sinetar from MIT found in the 1980s, they merely need the freedom to explore the topics that most interest them in the ways they want to (see Chapter 3).

For most of us, however, creativity is not something that we choose to give away lightly. There has to be some reward or recognition in prospect. Just as the Victoria Cross in the UK is granted to soldiers who demonstrate courage "above and beyond the cause of duty," so organizations need to demonstrate that they recognize that creativity is a gift of the individual "above and beyond the expectations of the job description."

Money is one incentive. Nortel Networks (see Chapter 7) offers substantial cash bonuses to those scientific staff who register patents that extend or protect the intellectual property of the organization.

But they couple it with a ceremony in a place of scientific interest and publicize the achievement in both their own internal house newsletters and intranets and in the local press. This form of recognition "validates" the financial reward, illustrating that it is for more than simple hard work and that the individual has given the company something unique to him or her.

Putting it at its simplest, unless you are so turned on by the nature of your work that exploring new ideas is a reward in itself, original insights and ideas are a negotiable asset. Most people will only give out if they feel they will get back. The return may be something as simple as straight cash but it is more often a sense of being valued and recognized and a consequent opening up of new career and work opportunities.

Q5: What makes a team creative?

A: Diversity, intellectual engagement, effective brainstorming, and constructive tension. The leading expert in this field, Dorothy Leonard of Harvard Business School (see Chapter 8), stresses that members need to be selected from their diversity in both "deep knowledge" and their intellectual and cultural way of thinking.

At the design company IDEO (see Chapter 6), teams are encouraged to question any and all assumptions, whether made by the company, clients, or the industry. They are expected to make mistakes often and early. Coming to the "right" solution too quickly is discouraged. Wild and visually expressed ideas are the order of the day, to get people thinking "out of their box."

Team leaders help to ensure this way of working is sustained. During the design of the new British Airways Waterside headquarters (see Chapter 6), the project manager made sure everybody had the opportunity to contribute to team discussion and brainstorms, even if this meant letting the timetable slip.

Q6: What makes an individual creative?

A: Questioning and open mind. The physicist turned management guru Danah Zohar (see Chapter 8) argues that people who demonstrate a high level of "spiritual intelligence" are more open to diversity; have a greater tendency to ask "why" and seek fundamental answers;

and have the capacity to face and use adversity. They actively seek uncomfortable situations because they recognize that their ability to interpret the environment around them will be enhanced as a result. They are always ready to challenge existing ideas and orthodoxies.

Well, this is of course an ideal. Few people actively seek out uncomfortable situations deliberately as a form of personal development. But a higher proportion of us learn from situations that are thrust upon us. Certainly the ability to see situations from a different perspective was a common feature of the managers we interviewed with the most successful track record in creative thought (see Chapter 8).

With this end in mind, it has become fashionable to publish books that enable managers to seek business answers from historical or philosophical figures as diverse as the Chinese general Sun Tzu, the Roman sage Marcus Aurelius, the British playwright William Shakespeare, and the French novelist Marcel Proust.

But once again, the importance of an open mind comes into play here. What conclusions and lessons you draw about business strategy from the reflections of a Chinese general written 2000 or more years ago may be different from what others read into the same text. They are not always universally applicable and the benefit is personal and not easily transferable.

So the message we would like to convey is: learn whatever you can from any source or experience you can. But bear in mind that the conclusions and insights that result are unique to you and can only be transferred to others as a proposition, not a dogma.

Q7: Can you be creative over the Net?

A: Yes and no, or even yes or no. Even as recently as five years ago, the general view was that while exchanges by e-mail or over company intranets could sustain an existing business relationship, the foundation for that relationship had to have been laid through face-to-face contact.

Now opinion is more divided. Research by the Massachusetts Institute of Technology (see Chapter 8 of the ExpressExec title *The Innovative Individual*) shows that electronic brainstorming can result in a more creative output than its face-to-face counterpart because the less assertive but equally creative participants had more of an opportunity to make a contribution.

Innovative companies like the historical games manufacturer GMT Games (see Chapter 4) have revolutionized their product development through personal and interactive exchanges with customers worldwide on their Website. It is still not clear whether there is a fundamental need for "tacit" contact between humans to establish the trust and intimacy that makes creativity possible, but a new generation of workers who have handled computers since they were in diapers is certainly shifting the boundaries. It all comes down to how comfortable you are with the technology.

Q8: Can you train someone to be creative?

A: This is a bit like the last question. Ten years ago, the general consensus would have been that you couldn't. Today, things have moved on.

First, we know a lot more about how the creative process works. In brainstorming, we know that there are certain things that encourage a free flow of ideas: the use of wild insights, visual imagery, and reverse logic, for example. And we know what discourages creativity: black-and-white thinking, too much analysis, and early attempts to pin things down (see Chapter 6). We also know that people do not usually think up their best ideas in a busy, stressful atmosphere and that the best ideas are often those that draw on insights and perspectives that are not work-related.

Second, there has been a revolution in the way training and development is conducted. Ten years ago, it focused principally on supporting what people do. Now it is used primarily to help shape how they think, feel and see. Exposing people to new ideas or activities to open up their minds and then discussing how the feelings or insights relate to their work has become commonplace. Teaching people specific techniques on how to brainstorm effectively is no more difficult that teaching them other teamworking skills (see the IDEO example in Chapter 6).

Q9: How do organizations lose their creativity?

A: By losing touch with the past, present, and future. They lose touch with the past when the people who pioneered new thinking move on and when new concepts become inviolable orthodoxies. They lose touch with the present and future when activities designed to keep them in touch with developments around them (attending conferences, benchmarking exercises, professional networking) fall out of use; or when, as Harvard's Dorothy Leonard stresses (see Chapter 8), their choice of senior managers is so homogeneous that they interpret external signals or developments through a "cognitive" filter.

Q10: How can organizations sustain creativity in a recession?

A: Since the failings described in the previous response happen most commonly during an economic downturn, this is the time when organizations need to take most care. In the last recession, large corporations like IBM and Marks & Spencer, which had dominated their industries in the 1980s, survived the downturn only to find a different world when the recovery took hold (see Chapter 1).

Three ways in which the trap can be avoided are ensuring that the thinking that led to creative breakthroughs is properly recorded through the use of new discussional software; buying back people on a flexible basis who were involved in this thinking on a flexible basis; and ensuring that any cutback in training does not affect events designed to keep the organization in touch with changes that are likely to affect their industries.

Index